2nd EDITION

# Pupil Book 3B

Series Editor: Peter Clarke

Authors: Elizabeth Jurgensen, Jeanette Mumford, Sandra Roberts

# Contents

# 3-digit numbers

## Recognise the place value of each digit in a 3-digit number

**Challenge 1**

**1** Write the numbers shown by the Base 10.

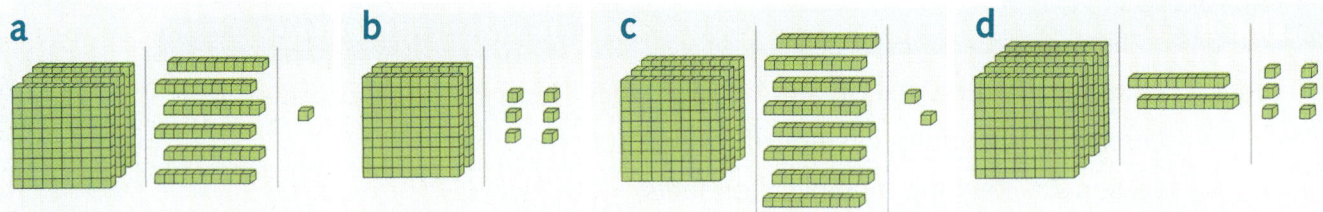

**You will need:**
- Base 10

a     b     c

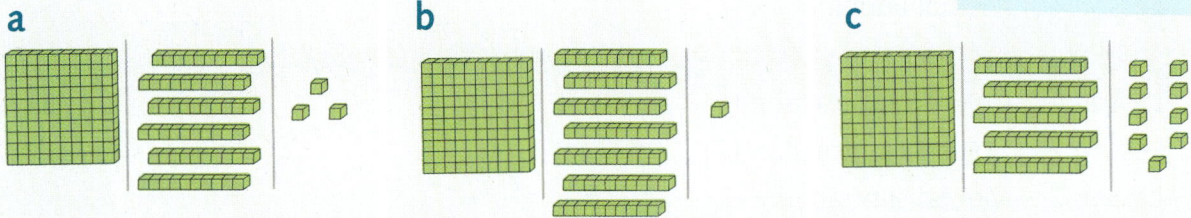

**2** Use Base 10 to make the numbers below.

a   126    b   164    c   119    d   237    e   242    f   266

**Challenge 2**

**1** Write the numbers shown by the Base 10.

a     b     c     d

**2** Write the numbers that have been partitioned into 100s, 10s and 1s.

a   200 + 10 + 9     b   400 + 50 + 5     c   500 + 70 + 9

d   600 + 20 + 9     e   700 + 70 + 3     f   800 + 8

**Challenge 3**

**1** Write the numbers that have been decomposed into 100s, 10s and 1s.

a   80 + 500 + 3     b   4 + 800 + 30     c   10 + 500 + 1

d   900 + 9 + 30     e   70 + 800 + 4     f   80 + 700 + 6

**2** I'm thinking of a number. The 100s digit is between 4 and 6, the 10s digit is 7 and the 1s digit is an odd number. Write as many possible answers as you can.

# Ordering numbers to 1,000

Compare and order numbers up to 1,000

**llenge 1**

Order each set of numbers, smallest to largest.

a   254, 168, 517, 429    b   572, 266, 103, 381    c   467, 236, 423, 351

d   109, 541, 377, 218    e   276, 317, 180, 441    f   288, 371, 125, 452

g   151, 132, 169, 124    h   183, 137, 142, 193    i   258, 231, 227, 263

j   238, 254, 286, 207    k   283, 253, 213, 243    l   376, 384, 362, 390

**llenge 2**

**1**  Write each set of numbers in ascending order.

a   265, 832, 163, 589, 322          b   831, 538, 529, 187, 276

c   945, 276, 254, 723, 433          d   376, 512, 352, 589, 312

e   478, 492, 382, 319, 408          f   821, 903, 962, 855, 965

g   444, 402, 414, 490, 476          h   899, 843, 856, 809, 819

**2**  For each number, write a 3-digit number that is larger and one that is smaller.

a   456    b   378    c   245    d   890

e   799    f   802    g   921    h   943

**llenge 3**

**1**  Write a set of instructions for ordering 3-digit numbers.

**2**  Using these digit cards, write two 3-digit numbers that are larger than the number on each of the whiteboards above.

2   5   8   9

5

# Using money to show 3-digit numbers

## Compose and decompose numbers using money

**Challenge 1**

What amounts are shown here? Write each answer as pence.

a 10p 10p 10p 1p 1p 1p 1p

b 10p 10p 10p 10p 1p 1p 1p

c 10p 10p 10p 10p 10p 1p

d 10p 10p 1p 1p 1p 1p 1p

e 10p 10p 10p 10p 1p 1p 1p 1p 1p 1p 1p

f £1 10p 10p 1p 1p 1p    g £1 10p 10p 10p 1p 1p 1p

h £1 £1 10p 10p 10p 1p    i £1 £1 10p 10p 1p 1p 1p 1p 1p 1p

**Example**

£1 + 10p + 10p + 10p + 10p + 1p = 141p

**Challenge 2**

1 What amounts are shown here? Write each answer as pence.

a £1 £1 10p 10p 10p 1p 1p 1p

b £1 £1 10p 10p 10p 10p 1p 1p 1p 1p 1p

c £1 £1 £1 10p 10p 1p 1p 1p 1p

d £1 £1 £1 £1 10p 10p 10p 10p 1p 1p

e £1 £1 £1 £1 £1 10p 10p 10p 10p 10p    f £1 £1 £1 £1 £1 £1 10p 1p 1p 1p

**Example**

£1 + £1 + 10p + 10p + 1p = 221p

2 What coins would you need to make these amounts?

a 245p    b 316p    c 453p    d 507p    e 732p    f 663p

**Challenge 3**

Imagine you had 8 coins in your pocket – they could be £1 coins, 10p coins or 1p coins. What amount of money might you have? Find different amounts.

**Example**

£1 + £1 + £1 + 10p + 10p + 10p + 1p + 1p = 332p

6

# Get the order

## Compare and order numbers up to 1,000

Work in threes.

- One player secretly writes a number on each of the pieces of paper.
- The other two players write the numbers 1–6 as a list in their books. At the top of the page, write: 'largest' and at the bottom write: 'smallest'.
- The player with the numbers reads them out one at a time.
- The other players decide where to write the number on their list.
- Players keep going until all the numbers have been read out.
- If a number cannot be put in order, write it next to the list.

**Challenge 1**

1 Secretly write a 2-digit number on each of the six pieces of paper.

2 How many of the numbers are in order?

3 Play again, this time with a different player writing the six secret numbers.

**You will need:**
- six small pieces of paper

**Challenge 2**

1 Secretly write a 3-digit number on each of the six pieces of paper.

2 Explain how you made your choices about where to write the numbers.

3 How can you improve your ordering next time?

**You will need:**
- six small pieces of paper

**Challenge 3**

1 Secretly write a 3-digit number on each of the ten pieces of paper. The other players write the numbers 1-10 as a list.

2 Which numbers did you find hardest to order? Explain why.

3 Write three top tips for playing this game. Try them out in the next round.

**You will need:**
- ten small pieces of paper

7

# Café totals

## Add amounts of money

How much would it cost to buy these items from the café?

**Challenge 1**

a   apple juice and fairy cake

b   orange juice and banana

c   pastry and apple juice

d   cheese sandwich and banana

e   orange juice and fairy cake

f   pastry and banana

apple juice 34p

orange juice 37p

cheese sandwich 58p

pastry 45p

fairy cake 42p

banana 25p

**Challenge 2**

a   cup of tea and tuna sandwich

b   ice cream and cheese toastie

c   apple pie and cup of tea

d   tuna sandwich and apple pie

e   ice cream and cheese toastie

f   apple pie and ice cream

apple pie 50p

cheese toastie 80p

ice cream 72p

tuna sandwich 74p

cup of tea 65p

**Challenge 3**

1   a   egg sandwich and mango juice

b   cheese toastie and milkshake

c   hot chocolate and egg sandwich

d   carrot cake and mango juice

e   egg sandwich and cheese toastie

f   milkshake and carrot cake

fruit salad 92p

hot chocolate 84p

mango juice 90p

milkshake 73p

carrot cake £1.28

egg sandwich 95p

cheese toastie 96p

2   I bought three things in the café. I spent a total of £2.96. What did I buy?

# Café change

## Subtract amounts of money to give change

| | | | |
|---|---|---|---|
| mini pizza 84p | carrot cake £1.28 | apple juice 34p | fairy cake 42p |
| ice cream 72p | cheese toastie 96p | orange juice 37p | banana 25p |
| cup of tea 65p | | tuna sandwich 74p | fruit salad 92p |
| milkshake 73p | slice of toast 21p | pastry 45p | hot chocolate 84p |

**Challenge 1**

Daniel has 50p. How much change will he get if he buys these items at the café?

   a   apple juice         b   banana         c   fairy cake

   d   slice of toast      e   pastry         f   orange juice

**Challenge 2**

1  Youssef has £1 (100p). How much change will he get if he buys these items?

   a   fairy cake         b   cup of tea       c   mini pizza

   d   ice cream         e   tuna sandwich    f   apple juice

2  Explain how to find change.

**Challenge 3**

1  Irene has £2 (200p). How much change will she get if she buys these items?

   a   fruit salad         b   orange juice      c   cheese toastie

   d   hot chocolate     e   carrot cake       f   milkshake

2  How much change will Sam get from £2 (200p) if she buys these items?

   a   orange juice and carrot cake      b   hot chocolate and cheese toastie

   c   milkshake and fruit salad

# Buying fruit

## Add and subtract amounts of money

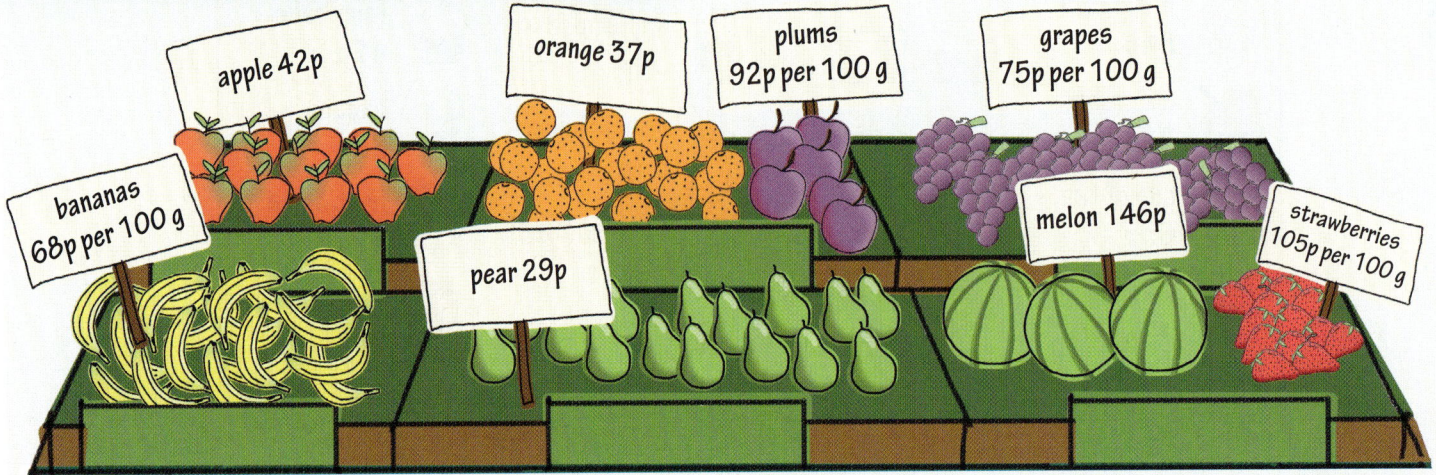

apple 42p

orange 37p

plums
92p per 100 g

grapes
75p per 100 g

bananas
68p per 100 g

pear 29p

melon 146p

strawberries
105p per 100 g

**Challenge 1**

You have £1 (100p). How much change will you get if you buy this fruit?

| | | |
|---|---|---|
| a  1 orange | b  100 g of grapes | c  1 apple |
| d  100 g of plums | e  1 apple and 1 orange | f  2 pears |
| g  1 pear and 1 orange | h  2 apples | i  2 oranges |

**Challenge 2**

You have £2 (200p). How much change will you get if you buy this fruit?

| | |
|---|---|
| a  1 melon | b  100 g of strawberries |
| c  1 orange and 1 apple | d  200 g of grapes |
| e  100 g of plums and a pear | f  200 g of bananas |
| g  1 melon and 1 orange | h  100 g of strawberries and 100 g of grapes |

**Challenge 3**

You have £5 (500p). How much change will you get if you buy this fruit?

| | |
|---|---|
| a  200 g of strawberries | b  1 melon and 1 orange |
| c  100 g of strawberries and 100 g of plums | d  2 melons |
| e  1 apple and 100 g of bananas | f  200 g of plums |
| g  3 apples | h  300 g of grapes |

# Furniture shopping

- Add and subtract amounts of money
- Solve word problems involving money and reason mathematically

Mina, Lily and Jacob are buying new items for their bedrooms. Mina has £100, Jacob has £200 and Lily has £500 to spend.

Work out these money problems. Show your working out.

**Challenge 1**

a  Jacob buys a rug and a mirror. How much does he spend?

b  Lily chooses the most expensive item in the shop. How much does it cost?

c  Mina buys a desk. How much change will she get?

d  Lily buys a desk and a rug. How much do they cost?

**Challenge 2**

a  Mina wants a bookcase and a mirror. How much more money does she need?

b  Lily buys the two most expensive items. What will the total be?

c  Jacob chooses the cheapest item in the shop. How much change will he get?

d  Lily buys a rug, mirror and a desk. How much will she spend?

**Challenge 3**

a  Lily buys a bed and a mirror. How much change does she get?

b  Mina wants a bookcase and a wardrobe. How much more money does she need?

c  Jacob buys two rugs and a mirror. How much change will he get?

d  If Mina and Jacob put their money together, can they buy 3 armchairs?

11

# Drawing and naming shapes

## Draw and name 2-D shapes

**You will need:**
- Resource 21: 3 x 3 pinboards
- ruler

**Challenge 1**

**1** Name these shapes.

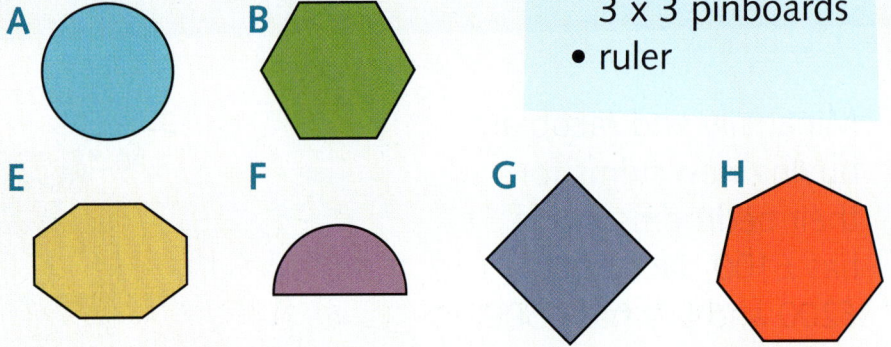

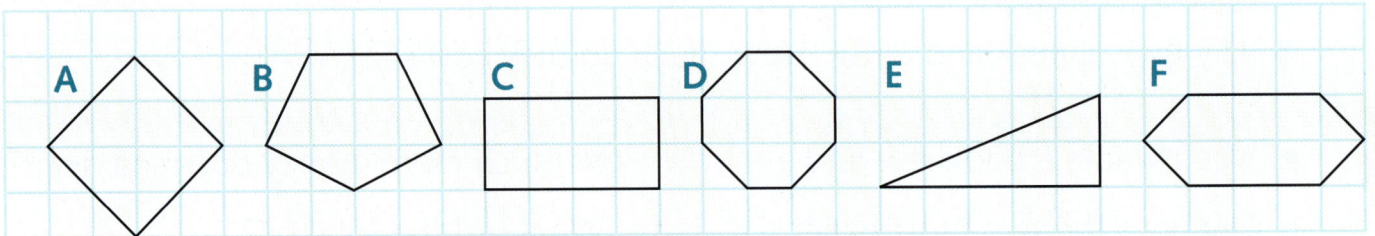

A    B

C    D    E    F    G    H

**2** Draw these shapes on the 3 x 3 pinboard.

   **a** triangle    **b** square    **c** rectangle    **d** pentagon    **e** hexagon

**Challenge 2**

**1** Name these shapes.

**You will need:**
- ruler
- squared paper

A    B    C    D    E    F

**2** Draw these shapes on squared paper.

   **a** a square with sides of 4 cm      **b** a rectangle with sides of 3 cm and 4 cm

   **c** 2 different pentagons          **d** 2 different hexagons

**Challenge 3**

Use the 3 x 3 pinboard to draw ten different 4-sided shapes.

**You will need:**
- Resource 21: 3 x 3 pinboards
- ruler

# Matching 2-D shapes

## Make shapes that match a property

**Challenge 1**

1 Using Resource 22: Matching shapes (1), join two triangles along matching edges to make these shapes.

a       b

**You will need:**
- Resource 22: Matching shapes (1)
- scissors
- squared paper
- ruler
- blue and red pencils

2 a Draw the two shapes above on squared paper.

   b Rule a blue line to show how the triangles fit together.

   c Circle the right angles in red.

**Challenge 2**

Work with a partner.

a Cut out the rectangle and two triangles on Resource 24: Matching shapes (2).

b Make the shapes below using the rectangle and the two right-angled triangles.

c Draw each shape showing how you made it using the rectangle and triangles.

**You will need:**
- Resource 24: Matching shapes (2)
- scissors
- squared paper
- ruler

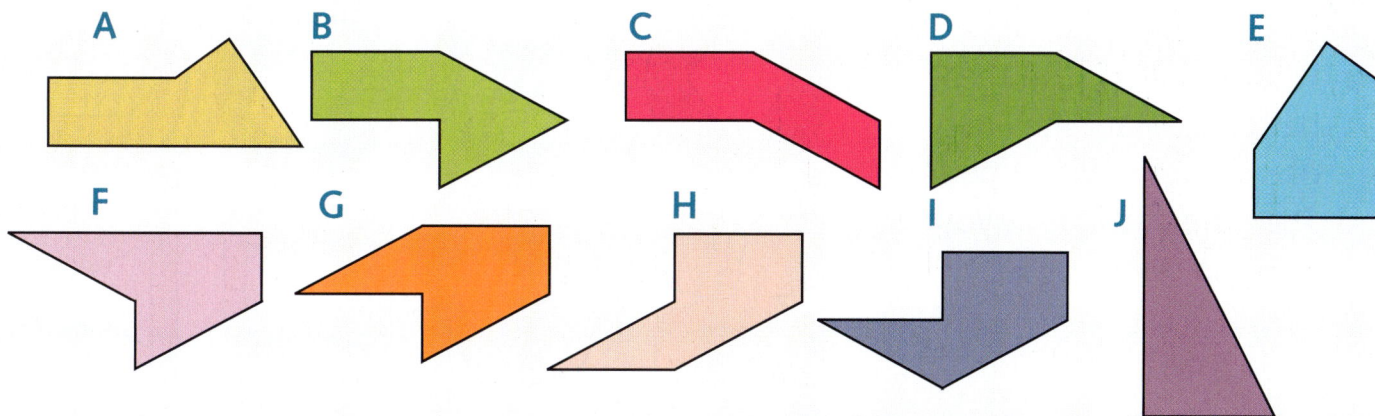

A   B   C   D   E

F   G   H   I   J

**Challenge 3**

Look at the ten shapes in Challenge 2. Copy and complete the table.

| Property | Shape |
|---|---|
| has one right angle | |
| has more than one right angle | A, |

13

# Paper shapes

## Make shapes using folding and cutting

**You will need:**
- paper squares and circles
- scissors
- ruler
- pen
- glue

**Challenge 1**

1  Fold the paper square into quarters.

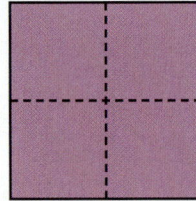

2  Make these patterns by folding and cutting. Mark the lines of symmetry with a pen. Stick the patterns in your exercise book.

a          b          c

 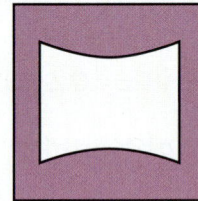 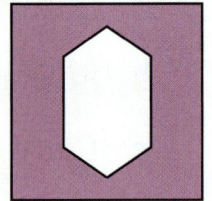

**Challenge 2**

1  Fold the paper circle and squares into quarters.

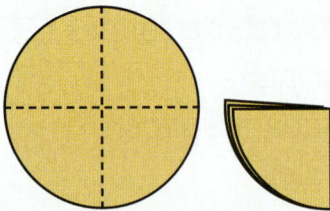     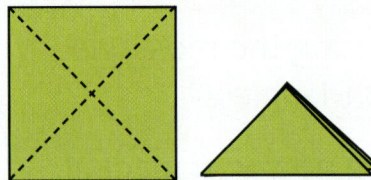     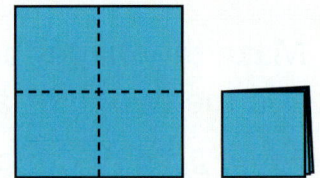

2  Find ways to make these patterns. Mark the lines of symmetry with a pen. Stick the patterns in your exercise book.

a          b          c          d

 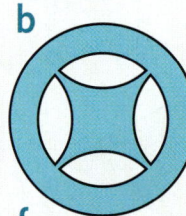 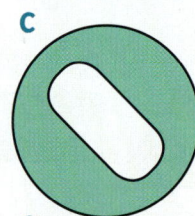 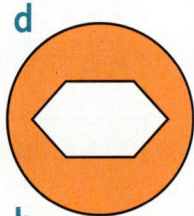

e          f          g          h

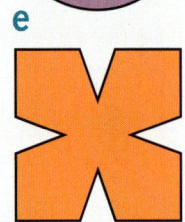 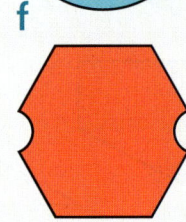  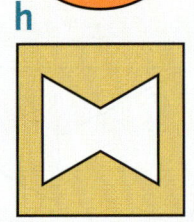

**Challenge 3**

Design two more patterns of your own. Mark any lines of symmetry and stick them in your exercise book.

# Properties of 2-D shapes

## Describe the properties of 2-D shapes

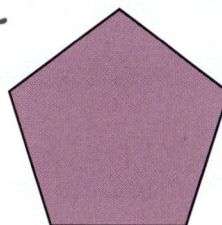

**Challenge 1**

Read the clues. Find the shape. Write its name.

a  I have 5 equal sides.

b  I have 1 right angle and 3 sides.

c  I have equal sides and 4 right angles.

d  I have 6 equal angles all greater than a right angle.

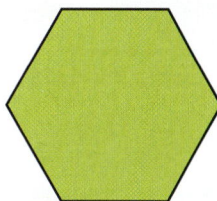

**Challenge 2**

1  Take two triangles and one regular shape from Resource 61: 2-D shapes. Fit them together to make these shapes. Name each shape.

**You will need:**
- Resource 61: 2-D shapes
- right-angle tester
- ruler
- scissors

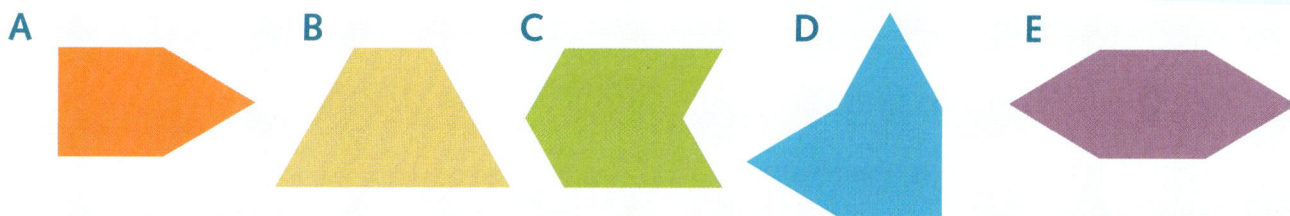

A    B    C    D    E

2  Solve these puzzles about the shapes in Question 1.

a  I have 2 angles greater than a right angle and 2 angles less than a right angle. Which shape am I?

b  I have 1 right angle and my 6 sides are equal in length. Which shape am I?

**Challenge 3**

Andy said, "I can use 12 rods to make 5 squares." Is he correct? Sketch the squares you make.

**You will need:**
- Twelve 10 rods from Base 10

# Counting in steps of 2, 4 and 8

## Count in multiples of 2, 4 and 8

**Challenge 1**

Write the missing numbers.

a   2, 4,      , 8,      ,      ,      ,      , 18,      ,      ,24

b   4,      ,      ,16,      ,      ,      ,      , 36,      , 44,

c   8,      , 24,      ,      ,      , 56,      ,      ,      , 88,

**Challenge 2**

**1** Find the multiples of each number and write them in order, smallest to largest.

a  multiples of 2    b  multiples of 4    c  multiples of 8

21  2  18
6  4  14
9  10  13

32  12  36
4  34  16
22  20  18

8  72  48
36  24  45
56  52  32

**2** Add the numbers to find the total.

a   2 + 4 + 4 =          b   2 + 4 + 8 =          c   4 + 4 + 8 =

d   8 + 8 + 4 + 4 =      e   2 + 8 + 8 + 2 + 8 + 2 =

f   4 + 4 + 8 + 8 + 2 + 8 + 4 =

**Challenge 3**

Read the clues to find the numbers.

a  We are multiples of 2, 4 and 8. We are between 20 and 50. We are

b  I am a multiple of 2, 4 and 8. I am less than 40. I have a 3 in the 10s place. I am

c  I am a multiple of 2, 4 and 8. I am also a multiple of 3. I am less than 40. I am

# Halving to find the division facts for the 4 multiplication table

## Use halving to recall the division facts for the 4 multiplication table

**Challenge 1**

Write the number that is half of each of these numbers.

| a | 24 | b | 46 | c | 38 | d | 64 | e | 88 | f | 16 |

| g | 36 | h | 18 | i | 62 | j | 32 | k | 48 | l | 44 |

**Challenge 2**

Divide each array by 4. Use the halve and halve again strategy to work out each answer. Write the division calculations for each array.

a 16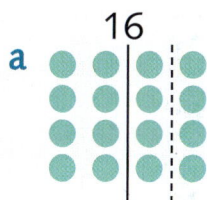

b 12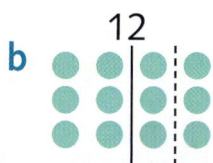

c 20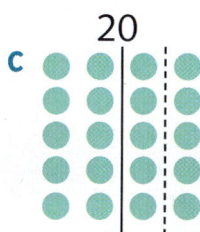

d 24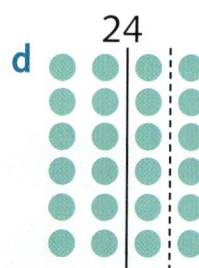

e 32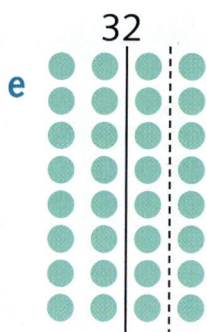

f 44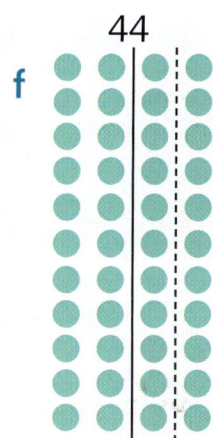

g 28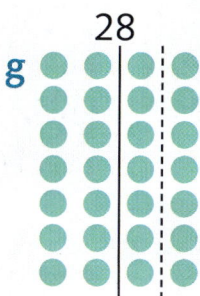

h 36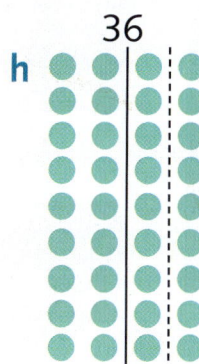

**Example**

48

48 ÷ 2 = 24

24 ÷ 2 = 12

So, 48 ÷ 4 = 12

**Challenge 3**

Answer these division facts using the halve and halve again strategy. Show your working.

a  60 ÷ 4 =

b  72 ÷ 4 =

c  64 ÷ 4 =

d  56 ÷ 4 =

e  76 ÷ 4 =

f  92 ÷ 4 =

# Halving to find the division facts for the 8 multiplication table

Use halving to recall the division facts for the 8 multiplication table

**Challenge 1**

Write the number that is half of these numbers, then halve the number again.

a  16     b  48     c  24     d  40     e  12

f  32     g  20     h  36     i  28     j  80

**Challenge 2**

Divide each array of chocolate bars by 8. Use the halve, halve again and then halve again strategy to work out each answer. Write the division calculations for each array.

**Example**

40

$40 \div 2 = 20$
$20 \div 2 = 10$
$10 \div 2 = 5$
So, $40 \div 8 = 5$

a  16

b  80

c  24

d  88

f  56

e  32

g  48

**Challenge 3**

Answer these division facts. Halve each number three times to find the answer. Show your working.

a  $112 \div 8 =$ ☐

b  $128 \div 8 =$ ☐

c  $104 \div 8 =$ ☐

d  $120 \div 8 =$ ☐

e  $144 \div 8 =$ ☐

f  $168 \div 8 =$ ☐

# Solving word problems (5)

## Solve word problems and reason mathematically

**Challenge 1**

Write the answers to these number facts.

a  $4 \times 8$    b  $6 \times 4$    c  $64 \div 8$    d  $36 \div 3$

e  $9 \times 4$    f  $72 \div 8$    g  $27 \div 3$    h  $9 \times 8$    i  $56 \div 8$

**Challenge 2**

Look at the drinks for sale.
Read each question below.
Decide which operation to use.
Write the calculation, then write
the answer to the problem.

£3

£4

£8

£16

a  Matt buys 7 single cups of juice.
How much does he pay?

b  Jim buys three 4-cup trays of juice
and 1 single cup of juice. How many
cups has he bought altogether?

c  Fran buys one 8-cup tray of juice.
How much does each cup cost?

d  Mary buys two 8-cup trays of juice
and 3 single cups of juice. How
much does she pay?

e  Jake wants to buy 25 cups of juice.
He has £50. Does he have enough
money? Explain your answer.

f  Is it better to buy four 2-cup trays
of juice or one 8-cup tray of juice?
Why?

**Challenge 3**

Use the pictures above to make up your own word problems with the
calculations below.

a  $6 \times 8 =$ ◯    b  $72 \div 8 =$ ◯    c  $(4 \times 3) + (1 \times 3) =$ ◯

d  $7 \times$ ◯ $= 28$    e  $(6 \times 2) + (3 \times 8) =$ ◯

# Fractions and division

Recognise, find and write unit fractions of a set of objects

**Challenge 1**

Find half of each set of stamps.

a

b

c

d

e

f

g

**Example**

$\frac{1}{2}$ of 6 = 3

**Challenge 2**

1 Find half of these numbers. Write your answer as a division calculation and as a fraction calculation.

a 14  b 18  c 24  d 28  e 34

f 36  g 40  h 46  i 42  j 54

**Example**

$12 \div 2 = 6$
$\frac{1}{2}$ of 12 = 6

2 Find a quarter of these numbers. Write your answer as a division calculation and as a fraction calculation.

a 12  b 20  c 24  d 32  e 40  f 48

**Example**

$12 \div 4 = 3$
$\frac{1}{4}$ of 12 = 3

3 Find a third of these numbers. Write your answer as a division calculation and as a fraction calculation.

a 18  b 27  c 36  d 21  e 42  f 48

**Example**

$24 \div 3 = 8$
$\frac{1}{3}$ of 24 = 8

4 Explain how you know what to divide by to find a fraction of any number.

**Challenge 3**

1 What fractions of each number can you find where the answer is a whole number? Write all the possibilities. Write your answers as a division calculation and as a fraction calculation.

a 15  b 20  c 24  d 27  e 32  f 40

2 Write three top tips for finding fractions of numbers.

# Fraction models

## Investigate non-unit fractions

**You will need:**
- coloured pencils
- squared paper

**Challenge 1**

1 Look at these models. Write the fractions that describe each model.

a

b

c

d

e

f

**Example**

$\frac{1}{6}$ blue and $\frac{5}{6}$ yellow

2 Draw your own models divided into 7 equal parts. Colour them in using 2 different colours. Write the fractions that describe each model.

**Challenge 2**

1 Look at these models. Write the fractions that describe each model.

a

b

c

d

e

f

g

h

i

2 Draw models divided into 10 equal parts. A model divided into 10 equal parts can be described using tenths. Colour the models in as many different ways as you can and write the fractions that describe each model.

**Challenge 3**

1 Take a handful of cubes in two different colours and use them to make a model. Draw the model. Write the fractions.

**You will need:**
- 20 interlocking cubes

2 Take a handful of cubes in three different colours and use them to make a model. Draw the model. Write the fractions.

# Ordering fractions

## Order unit fractions and fractions with the same denominator

**Challenge 1**

Write the fraction that describes the coloured part of each circle.

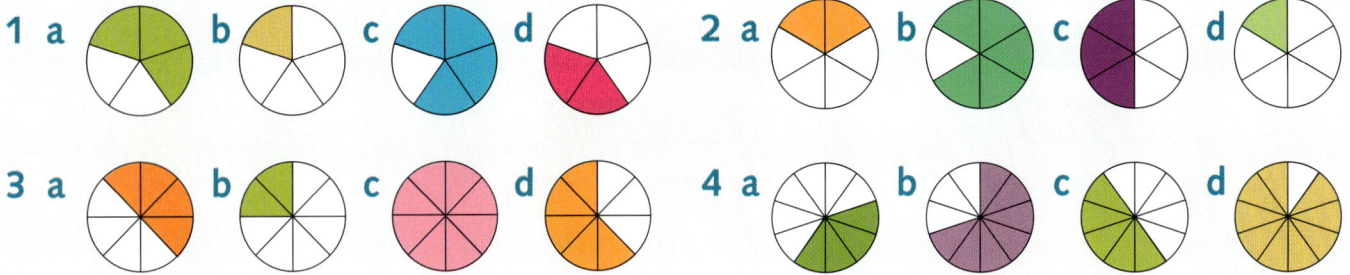

1 a    b    c    d      2 a    b    c    d

3 a    b    c    d      4 a    b    c    d

5   Now put each set of fractions in order, smallest to largest.

**Challenge 2**

1   Order each set of fractions, smallest to largest.

a   $\frac{3}{4}$   $\frac{1}{4}$   $\frac{2}{4}$   $\frac{4}{4}$       b   $\frac{3}{8}$   $\frac{6}{8}$   $\frac{1}{8}$   $\frac{2}{8}$

c   $\frac{4}{9}$   $\frac{8}{9}$   $\frac{2}{9}$   $\frac{5}{9}$       d   $\frac{4}{6}$   $\frac{2}{6}$   $\frac{5}{6}$   $\frac{6}{6}$

2   Write instructions for ordering fractions when the denominators are all the same.

3   Would you rather have $\frac{2}{8}$ or $\frac{5}{8}$ of a chocolate cake? Explain why.

**Challenge 3**

1   Order each set of fractions, smallest to largest.

a   $\frac{1}{4}$   $\frac{1}{2}$   $\frac{1}{10}$   $\frac{1}{5}$    b   $\frac{1}{6}$   $\frac{1}{7}$   $\frac{1}{2}$   $\frac{1}{3}$

c   $\frac{1}{9}$   $\frac{1}{4}$   $\frac{1}{6}$   $\frac{1}{12}$    d   $\frac{1}{17}$   $\frac{1}{3}$   $\frac{1}{5}$   $\frac{1}{11}$

2   Write instructions for ordering unit fractions.

3   What does the denominator tell us about the fraction?

# Fractions on number lines

## Write fractions on a number line

**Challenge 1**

Write the missing fractions on these number tracks.

**a**
0      1

**b**
0      $\frac{2}{4}$      1

**c**
0    $\frac{1}{5}$      $\frac{4}{5}$   1

**d**
0    $\frac{2}{6}$      1

**e**
0      $\frac{3}{7}$    $\frac{5}{7}$    1

**f**
0   $\frac{1}{8}$    $\frac{4}{8}$     1

**Challenge 2**

**1** Complete these fraction number lines.

**a** quarters   0      1

**b** thirds   0      1

**c** fifths   0      1

**d** eighths   0      1

**2** Write the next four fractions after 1.

**a** $\frac{3}{4}$, 1,    ,    ,    ,

**b** $\frac{4}{6}$, $\frac{5}{6}$, 1,    ,    ,    ,

**c** $\frac{6}{8}$, $\frac{7}{8}$, 1,    ,    ,    ,

**d** $\frac{2}{3}$, 1,    ,    ,    ,

**e** $\frac{8}{10}$, $\frac{9}{10}$, 1,    ,    ,    ,

**f** $\frac{7}{9}$, $\frac{8}{9}$, 1,    ,    ,    ,

**Challenge 3**

Draw two number lines and write these fractions on them.

**a** $\frac{1}{2}$, $\frac{1}{4}$, $\frac{3}{4}$, $\frac{1}{3}$, $\frac{2}{3}$

**b** $\frac{1}{2}$, $\frac{1}{4}$, $\frac{3}{4}$, $\frac{1}{8}$, $\frac{3}{8}$, $\frac{5}{8}$, $\frac{7}{8}$

# Measuring in centimetres

Use a ruler to draw and measure lines to the nearest centimetre

**Challenges 1, 2**

**You will need:**
• ruler

A
B
C
D
E

1 Measure the length of each line to the nearest centimetre. Copy and complete the table.

| Line | A | B | C | D | E |
|---|---|---|---|---|---|
| Length in cm | | | | | |

2 Draw lines that are 5 cm longer than lines A and B. Write the new length above the line.

3 Draw lines that are $2\frac{1}{2}$ cm shorter than lines C, D and E. Write the new length above the line.

**Challenge 3**

Henry said, "If I take a length of ribbon from each basket and sew them together, I can make 6 different lengths."

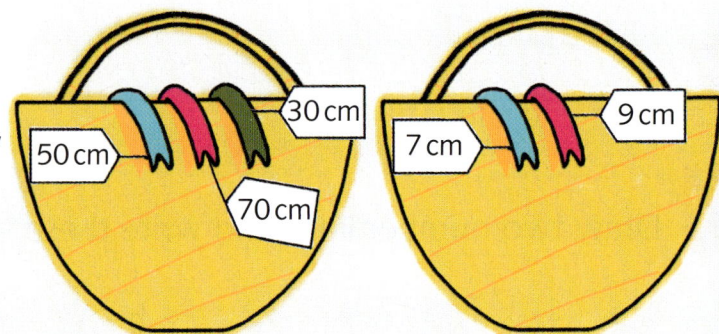

a Is he correct? Investigate.

b What is the longest length of ribbon he can make?

# Measuring in millimetres

Use a ruler to draw and measure lines to the nearest millimetre

**You will need:**
• ruler

**Challenge 1**

1  Draw lines of these lengths.

a  10 mm   b  30 mm   c  80 mm   d  55 mm   e  25 mm   f  75 mm

2  Measure these objects to the nearest millimetre.

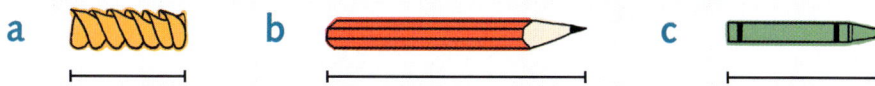

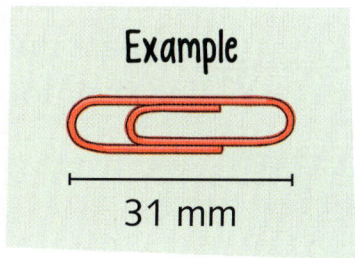

a   b   c

**Example**

31 mm

**Challenge 2**

1  Measure each rod in millimetres, then draw a line of the same length. Below the line, write the length in two ways.

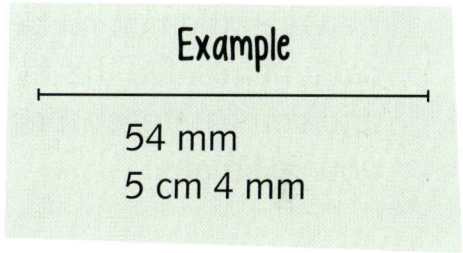

a
b
c
d
e

**Example**

54 mm
5 cm 4 mm

2  Draw lines of these lengths:

a   3 cm shorter than 85 mm      b   4 cm longer than 58 mm

**Challenge 3**

Amy needs 4 buttons of the same size. This is her collection of buttons. Which size of button does she choose?

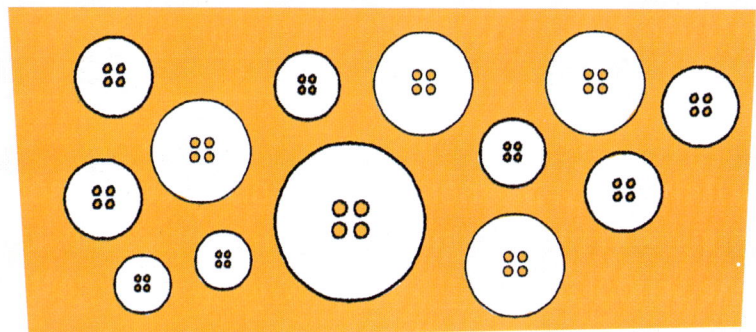

# Measuring and comparing lengths

## Measure and compare lengths and multiples of lengths in m and cm

**Challenge 1**

Work with a partner.
Find pairs of objects.
For each pair:
- measure and compare their lengths
- find their total length

**Example**

A     B

21 cm    28 cm

Book B is 7 cm longer than Book A.
The total length is 49 cm.

**You will need:**
- ruler
- measuring tape
- collection of objects to measure

**Challenge 2**

1  Work with a partner. Place the objects on the floor. Estimate, then measure the distance between them in metres and centimetres. Do this five times and compare each measure with your estimate.

**Example**

Estimate: 3 m 10 cm

3 m 35 cm

Measure: 3 m 35 cm

2  Jim stacks boxes in a warehouse. He has a delivery of three sizes of boxes. Find the total height when he makes a stack of 2, 4, 5 and 10 of each box. Copy and complete the table.

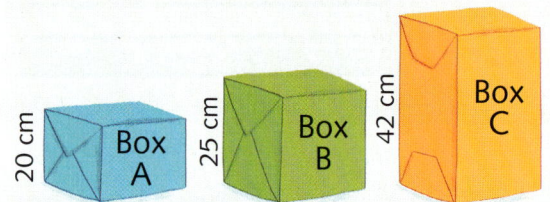

20 cm Box A    25 cm Box B    42 cm Box C

|  | 2 boxes | 4 boxes | 5 boxes | 10 boxes |
|---|---|---|---|---|
| Box A |  |  |  |  |
| Box B |  |  |  |  |
| Box C |  |  |  |  |

**Challenge 3**

Work with a partner. Find the distance, in metres, between different pairs of objects in the playground, for example, the school gate and the main door to the school building. Your teacher will suggest suitable things to measure.

# Adding and subtracting lengths

## Add and subtract length using mixed units

**Challenge 1**

Jim had four bendy straws, each 15 cm long.
He bent each straw to make two parts. He used
centimetres and millimetres to measure the parts.
Copy and complete his results.

a   9 cm +          cm = 15 cm

b   $7\frac{1}{2}$ cm +          cm = 15 cm

c   4 cm 5 mm +          cm          mm = 15 cm

d   12 cm 5 mm +          cm          mm = 15 cm

**Example**

7 cm

8 cm

8 cm + 7 cm = 15 cm

**Challenge 2**

R          S          T

1   Work out the length of Trucks R and T.

2   All three trucks board a ferry. They park
    behind each other nose to tail. What is
    their total length?

3   A van is half the length of Truck S. What is
    its length?

- Truck R is 2 m 30 cm
  shorter than Truck S

- Truck S is 8 m 40 cm

- Truck T is $\frac{1}{2}$ m longer
  than Truck S

**Challenge 3**

There are five trucks waiting to board the ferry. The scale
shows the height of each truck. Which truck is:

a   18 cm taller than Truck C?

b   25 cm short of 5 m?

c   26 cm shorter than Truck A?

d   What is the difference in height between Trucks A and E?

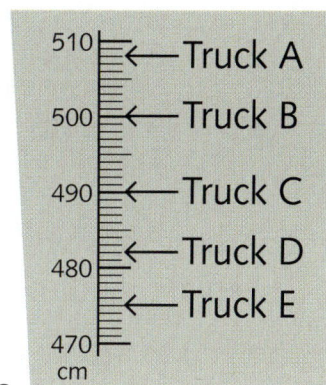

510 ←—Truck A

500 ←—Truck B

490 ←—Truck C

480 ←—Truck D

←—Truck E

470

cm

27

# Expanded addition

- Add 3-digit numbers using the expanded written method of column addition
- Estimate the answer to a calculation

**Challenge 1**

Use the expanded method to add these numbers together.

a   53 + 25      b   41 + 37      c   64 + 23

d   136 + 143    e   165 + 131    f   238 + 160

g   216 + 283    h   306 + 292

**Example**
```
  215
+ 342
-----
    7
   50
  500
-----
  557
```

**Challenge 2**

First estimate the answer to each calculation. Then use the expanded method to work out the answer.

a   285 + 417    b   258 + 431    c   392 + 307

d   445 + 313    e   427 + 436    f   308 + 395

g   417 + 387    h   226 + 479    i   516 + 247

**Example**

371 + 328

*300 add 300 is 600, and the 10s and 1s are nearly 100, so my estimate is 700.*

**Challenge 3**

**1** First estimate the answer to each calculation. Then use the expanded method to work out the answer.

a   406 + 389    b   517 + 378    c   605 + 389

d   468 + 474    e   547 + 463    f   738 + 255

g   179 + 808    h   643 + 397

**2** A pupil has written out this calculation.
Explain what needs to be changed in their working out.

```
  312
+ 437
-----
    9
    4
    7
-----
  749
```

# Column addition (1)

- Add 3-digit numbers using the formal written method of column addition
- Estimate the answer to a calculation

**Challenge 1**

**1** Use the expanded method to add these numbers together.

a  235 + 141   b  173 + 206   c  267 + 132

d  159 + 130   e  286 + 213   f  324 + 255

**Example**
```
  317
+ 361
    8
   70
  600
  678
```

**2** Work out these using the formal method.

a  153 + 232   b  275 + 213   c  241 + 356

d  374 + 223   e  261 + 327   f  321 + 264

**Example**
```
  317
+ 361
  678
```

**Challenge 2**

First estimate the answer to each calculation. Then use the formal method to work out the answer.

**1**  a  345 + 351   b  273 + 416   c  368 + 321   d  438 + 361

e  508 + 381   f  472 + 326   g  581 + 217   h  483 + 416

**2**  a  326 + 347   b  259 + 435   c  415 + 319   d  536 + 248

e  447 + 344   f  539 + 353   g  263 + 518   h  366 + 326

**Challenge 3**

**1** First estimate the answer to each calculation. Then use the formal method to work out the answer.

a  538 + 358   b  482 + 409   c  558 + 237   d  627 + 359

e  736 + 246   f  555 + 438   g  837 + 158   h  574 + 316

**2** Explain how to estimate the answers to addition calculations.

# Column addition (2)

- Add 3-digit numbers using the formal written method of column addition
- Estimate the answer to a calculation

**Challenge 1**

First estimate the answer to each calculation.
Then use the formal method to work out the answer.

| | | |
|---|---|---|
| **a** 153 + 146 | **b** 137 + 151 | **c** 264 + 125 |
| **d** 216 + 243 | **e** 357 + 221 | **f** 208 + 381 |
| **g** 362 + 316 | **h** 427 + 342 | **i** 415 + 363 |
| **j** 512 + 374 | **k** 206 + 681 | **l** 467 + 531 |

**Example**

```
  162
+ 237
-----
  399
```

**Challenge 2**

First estimate the answer to each calculation.
Then use the formal method to work out the answer.

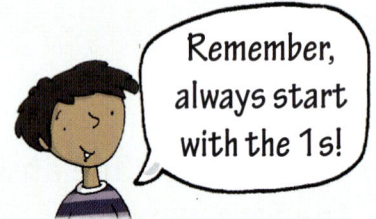

Remember, always start with the 1s!

**1**
| | | | |
|---|---|---|---|
| **a** 264 + 327 | **b** 339 + 346 | **c** 325 + 437 | **d** 529 + 338 |
| **e** 417 + 467 | **f** 574 + 318 | **g** 356 + 529 | **h** 608 + 388 |

**2**
| | | | |
|---|---|---|---|
| **a** 463 + 274 | **b** 532 + 394 | **c** 467 + 481 | **d** 573 + 345 |
| **e** 295 + 642 | **f** 485 + 361 | **g** 563 + 354 | **h** 492 + 485 |

**Challenge 3**

First estimate the answer to each calculation.
Then use the formal method to work out the answer.

**1**
| | | | |
|---|---|---|---|
| **a** 418 + 347 | **b** 562 + 374 | **c** 635 + 284 | **d** 381 + 409 |
| **e** 762 + 193 | **f** 574 + 372 | **g** 418 + 546 | **h** 719 + 159 |

**2**
| | | | |
|---|---|---|---|
| **a** 257 + 365 | **b** 362 + 359 | **c** 476 + 287 | **d** 658 + 176 |

# Mental addition

Add numbers mentally and use the inverse operation to check the answer

**Challenge 1**

Write 12 addition calculations using these numbers as addends.

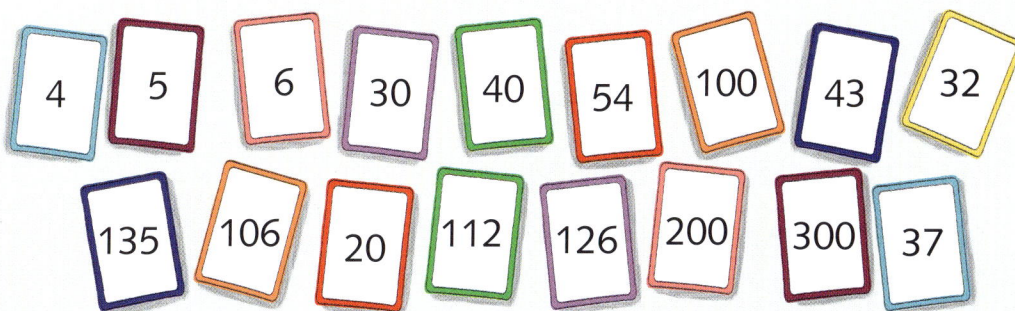

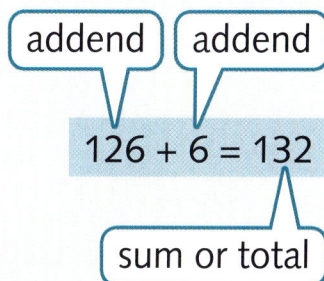

4  5  6  30  40  54  100  43  32

135  106  20  112  126  200  300  37

addend  addend

$126 + 6 = 132$

sum or total

**Challenge 2**

1  Write 12 addition calculations using these numbers as addends.

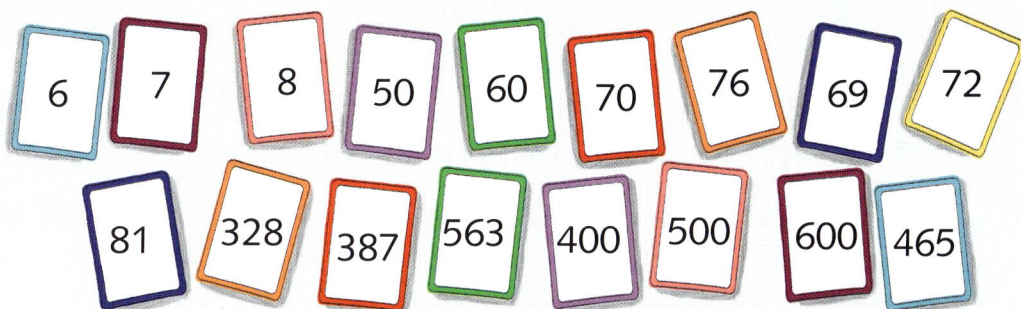

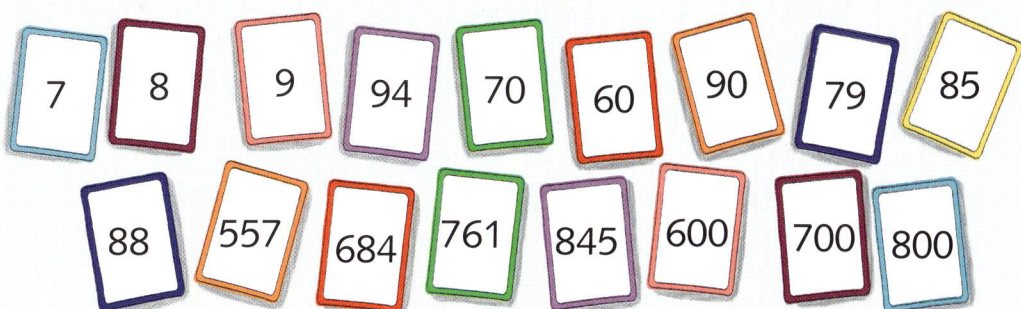

6  7  8  50  60  70  76  69  72

81  328  387  563  400  500  600  465

2  Choose four of your calculations and use subtraction to check the answers.

**Challenge 3**

1  Write 12 addition calculations using these numbers as addends.

7  8  9  94  70  60  90  79  85

88  557  684  761  845  600  700  800

2  Choose two different calculations that you can do mentally.
Explain what happens in your head when you work them out.

3  Choose four of your calculations and use subtraction to check the answers.

# Column subtraction (1)

- Subtract 3-digit numbers using the formal written method of column subtraction
- Estimate the answer to a calculation

**Challenge 1**

Work out these calculations using the formal method.

| | | |
|---|---|---|
| a  37 – 14 | b  58 – 45 | c  49 – 26 |
| d  63 – 31 | e  275 – 131 | f  264 – 142 |
| g  285 – 151 | h  297 – 165 | i  235 – 124 |
| j  265 – 143 | k  379 – 156 | l  368 – 234 |

**Example**

$$\begin{array}{r} 465 \\ -\ 213 \\ \hline 252 \end{array}$$

**Challenge 2**

First estimate the answer to each calculation.
Then use the formal method to work out the answer.

1
| | | | |
|---|---|---|---|
| a  457 – 236 | b  483 – 251 | c  548 – 313 | d  577 – 241 |
| e  476 – 124 | f  596 – 371 | g  485 – 223 | h  536 – 204 |

2
| | | | |
|---|---|---|---|
| a  372 – 135 | b  381 – 148 | c  394 – 278 | d  431 – 107 |
| e  463 – 217 | f  485 – 149 | g  566 – 338 | h  547 – 239 |

**Challenge 3**

1  First estimate the answer to each calculation.
   Then use the formal method to work out the answer.

| | | |
|---|---|---|
| a  583 – 267 | b  645 – 128 | c  696 – 358 |
| d  751 – 425 | e  736 – 329 | f  792 – 454 |
| g  863 – 517 | h  974 – 735 | |

2  Explain how to estimate the answers to subtraction calculations.

# Column subtraction (2)

- Subtract 3-digit numbers using the formal written method of column subtraction
- Estimate the answer to a calculation

**llenge 1**

First estimate the answer to each calculation.
Then use the formal method to work out the answer.

| | | | | | |
|---|---|---|---|---|---|
| a | 256 – 134 | b | 275 – 121 | c | 298 – 163 |
| d | 267 – 142 | e | 354 – 102 | f | 378 – 243 |
| g | 356 – 124 | h | 384 – 251 | i | 468 – 147 |

**Example**

$$478$$
$$-\ 353$$
$$\overline{125}$$

**llenge 2**

First estimate the answer to each calculation.
Then use the formal method to work out the answer.

1  a  273 – 145     b  361 – 227

   c  457 – 329     d  383 – 146

2  a  326 – 142     b  365 – 183     c  348 – 271     d  437 – 253

   e  516 – 372     f  538 – 276     g  657 – 382     h  614 – 283

**Example**

$$\overset{515}{6\cancel{5}8}$$
$$-\ 274$$
$$\overline{384}$$

**llenge 3**

First estimate the answer to each calculation.
Then use the formal method to work out the answer.

1  a  439 – 256     b  518 – 353     c  654 – 217     d  582 – 355

   e  464 – 231     f  627 – 156     g  758 – 429     h  708 – 341

2  a  432 – 156     b  547 – 268     c  642 – 374     d  675 – 297

   e  773 – 212     f  857 – 479     g  863 – 584     h  815 – 639

# Mental subtraction

Subtract numbers mentally and use the inverse operation to check the answer

**Challenge 1**

Write 12 subtraction calculations using these numbers as the minuend and subtrahend.

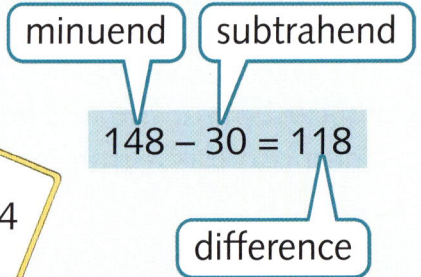

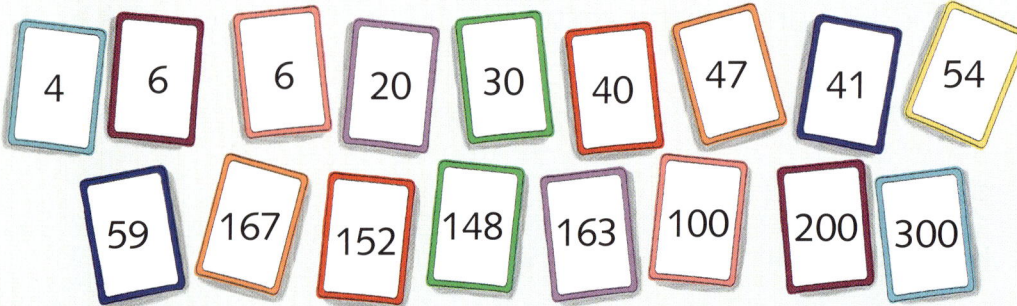

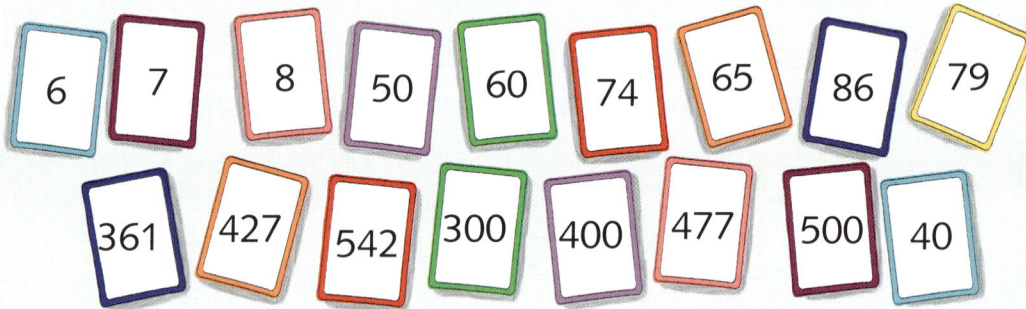

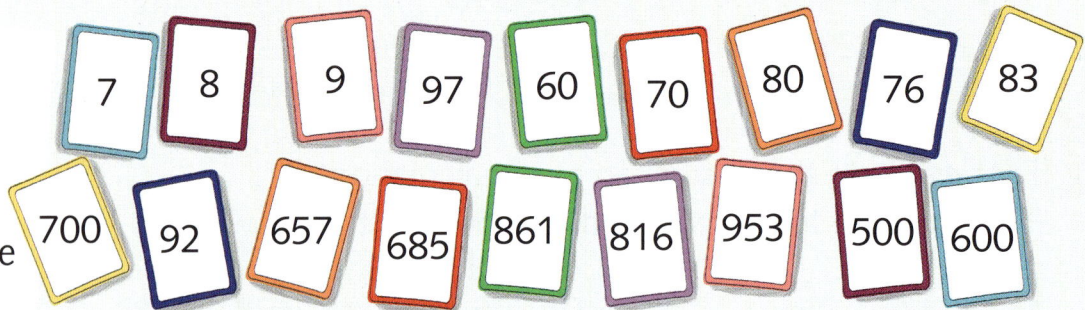

minuend    subtrahend

$148 - 30 = 118$

difference

4   6   6   20   30   40   47   41   54

59   167   152   148   163   100   200   300

**Challenge 2**

1 Write 12 subtraction calculations using these numbers as the minuend and subtrahend.

6   7   8   50   60   74   65   86   79

361   427   542   300   400   477   500   40

2 Choose four of your calculations and use addition to check the answers.

**Challenge 3**

1 Write 12 subtraction calculations using these numbers as the minuend and subtrahend.

7   8   9   97   60   70   80   76   83

700   92   657   685   861   816   953   500   600

2 Choose two different calculations that you can do mentally. Explain what happens in your head when you work them out.

3 Choose four of your calculations and use addition to check the answers.

# Sports shop spending

- Add and subtract amounts of money
- Solve word problems involving money and reason mathematically

Work out these money problems. Show your working out.

£125  £68  £348  £90  £253  £500

**Marcia has £100.
Oliver has £200.
Laura has £500.**

**Challenge 1**

a  Marcia buys a tennis racquet. How much change will she get?

b  Oliver buys a tennis racquet and some trainers. How much does he spend?

c  Laura needs a tennis racquet for herself and one for her sister. How much money does she need?

d  Laura buys a cricket bat and a scooter. How much does she need to pay?

**Challenge 2**

a  Oliver buys a tennis racquet and some trainers. How much does he spend?

b  Laura buys a skateboard. How much change will she get?

c  Oliver buys the cheapest item in the shop. How much change will he get?

d  Oliver wants two cricket bats. How much more money will he need?

**Challenge 3**

a  Laura buys a skateboard and a helmet. The cost comes to £479. What was the price of the helmet?

b  If Oliver and Laura put their money together and bought a skateboard and a scooter, how much change would they get?

c  Oliver buys a tennis racquet and some tennis shoes. He spends £128. What was the cost of the tennis shoes?

d  Imagine you had £500 to spend. What items would you buy?

# Tally charts

Interpret and present data using tables and charts

**Challenge 1**

**1** George made a table for the types of vehicles passing his school at lunchtime. Copy and complete the table.

| Vehicle | Number | Total |
|---|---|---|
| car | IIIIIIIIIIIIII | |
| bus | IIIIIIIIIIII | |
| bicycle | IIIIIIIII | |
| lorry or van | IIIIIIIIII | |
| motorbike | IIIIIII | |

**2 a** Copy and complete the tally chart below. Use the totals that George found in Question 1. Draw the tally marks and write the totals in the Frequency column.

| Vehicle | Tally | Frequency |
|---|---|---|
| car | | |
| bus | | |
| bicycle | | |
| lorry or van | | |
| motorbike | | |

**Remember**

IIII stands for 5

**b** How many vehicles were two-wheeled?

**c** How many more cars were there than buses?

**d** Write two statements about the data shown in the table.

**1** Donna asked some people, "Where do you go to buy your fruit and vegetables?" She made a tally chart for their responses.

| Location | Tally | Frequency |
|---|---|---|
| supermarket | ⅲⅲ ⅲⅲ ⅲⅲ ⅲⅲ ⅲ | |
| corner shop | ⅲⅲ ⅲⅲ ⅰ | |
| market stall | ⅲⅲ ⅲⅲ ⅲⅲ | |
| greengrocer | ⅲⅲ ⅲⅲ ⅱ | |

**a** Copy the tally chart. Count the tally marks. Write the totals in the Frequency column.

**b** Where do most people buy their fruit and vegetables?

**c** Which is the least popular location?

**d** How many more people shopped at the supermarket than at the market stall?

**e** How many people did Donna ask altogether?

**1** Donna asked some other people, "What kind of bread do you prefer?"

| Bread | Tally | Frequency |
|---|---|---|
| white | | 18 |
| brown | | 21 |
| sourdough | | 10 |
| bloomer | | 6 |
| naan | | 5 |

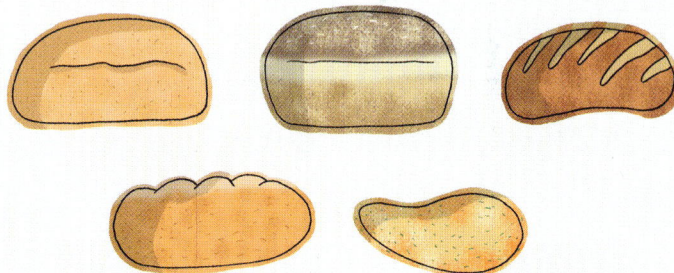

**a** Copy the table and complete the Tally column.

**b** What is the most popular type of bread?

**c** How many more people prefer white bread to sourdough?

**2** Write two statements about the data shown in your table.

**3** Look at George's chart in Challenge 1. How might the chart be different if he had collected his data at 6:00 a.m.? Give a reason for your answer.

# Charity pictograms

Interpret and present data in pictograms where one picture represents 2 units

**You will need:**
- squared paper
- ruler

**Challenge 1**

1  Sam collected this money for charity.

Copy this pictogram.
Count each type of coin.
Complete the pictogram.

**Coins collected for charity**

| | | | | |
|---|---|---|---|---|
| 1p | | | | |
| 2p | | | | |
| 5p | | | | |
| 10p | | | | |

**Number of coins**

**Key**

● 2 coins
◖ 1 coin

2  Use the information to answer these questions.

a  How many 5p coins were collected?

b  Which is the least common coin?

c  How many coins were collected altogether?

d  How many coins are:

i silver?          ii copper?

**1** Class 3A collected these coins for charity.

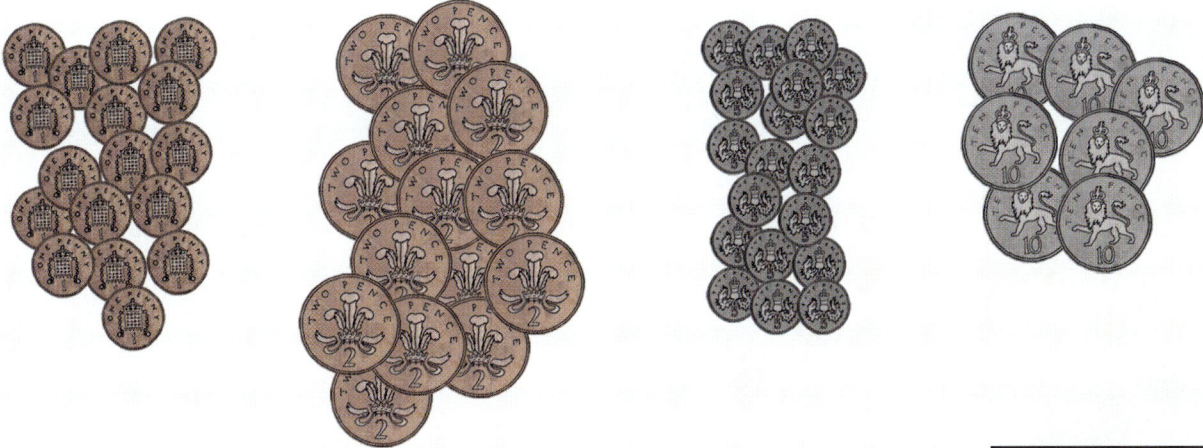

**a** Count each type of coin and write the total in the table.

**b** Copy and complete the pictogram.

**Coins collected for charity**

| | | | | | | | | | |
|---|---|---|---|---|---|---|---|---|---|
| 1p | | | | | | | | | |
| 2p | | | | | | | | | |
| 5p | | | | | | | | | |
| 10p | | | | | | | | | |

**Number of coins**

| Coin | Number |
|---|---|
| 1p | |
| 2p | |
| 5p | |
| 10p | |

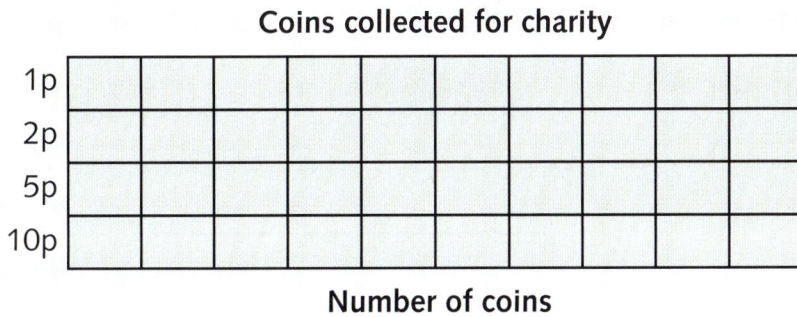

**Key**

● 2 coins

◖ 1 coin

**2** Use the information to answer these questions.

**a** How many 5p coins were collected?

**b** Which is the least common coin?

**c** How many coins were collected altogether?

**d** How many more 2p coins than 10p coins were collected?

**1** Draw a pictogram to show what Class 3A collected the next week.

| Coin | 1p | 2p | 5p | 10p | 20p |
|---|---|---|---|---|---|
| Number | 16 | 12 | 8 | 14 | 7 |

**2** Write two statements about the data displayed in your pictogram.

# Picnic bar charts

Interpret and present data in bar charts with intervals labelled in multiples of 2

cherries

raisins

biscuits

sandwiches

**You will need:**
- squared paper
- ruler
- coloured pencils

1 Count each item of picnic food.
Copy and complete the tally chart.

| Item | Tally | Frequency |
|------|-------|-----------|
| sandwiches | | |
| biscuits | | |
| cherries | | |
| raisins | | |

2 Copy and complete the bar chart.

3 a What does the tallest bar show?

  b How many more sandwiches
were there than:

    i    biscuits?

    ii   packs of raisins?

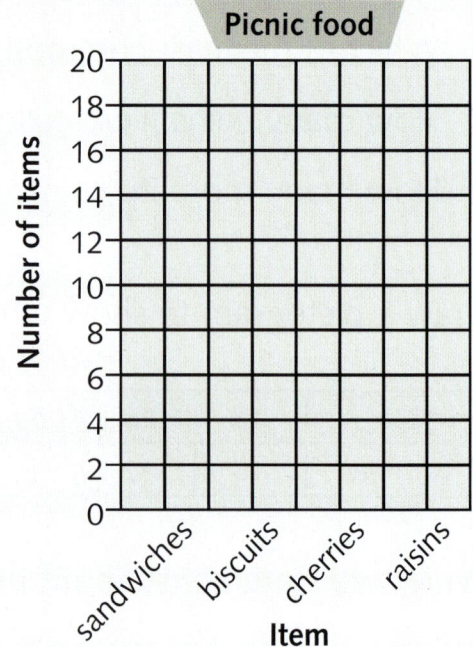

Picnic food

**1** Copy and complete the table for the number of each type of sandwich.

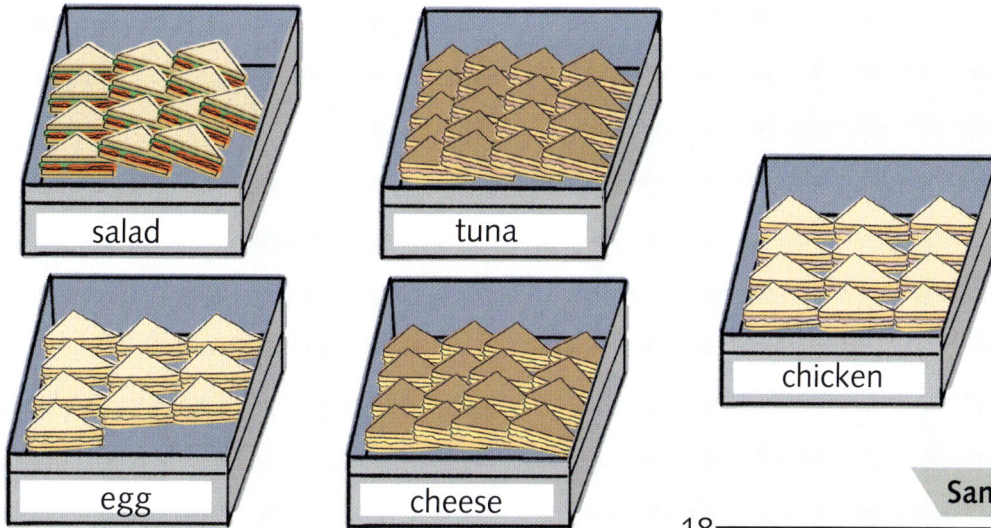

| Sandwich | Frequency |
|----------|-----------|
| salad | |
| tuna | |
| egg | |
| cheese | |
| chicken | |

salad

tuna

chicken

egg

cheese

**2** Copy and complete the bar chart.

**3** Which sandwich was:

**a** the most popular?

**b** the least popular?

**Sandwich fillings**

Number of sandwiches

18
16
14
12
10
8
6
4
2
0

salad    tuna    egg    cheese    chicken

**Type of sandwich**

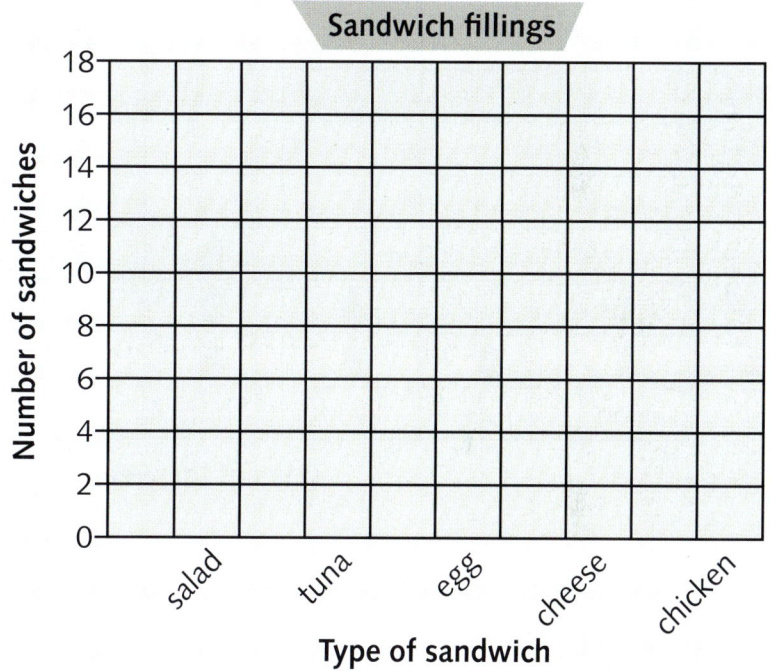

**4** How many more tuna sandwiches were made than:

**a** salad?    **b** cheese?    **c** chicken?    **d** egg?

Janice asked 50 children how they liked their eggs prepared.

**a** Use this information to make a bar chart and a pictogram of her results.

**b** Write three statements describing her results.

| Eggs | Frequency |
|------|-----------|
| boiled | 8 |
| fried | 14 |
| poached | 17 |
| scrambled | 11 |

# Pictograms and bar charts

Use information presented in scaled pictograms, bar charts and tables to answer questions

**You will need:**
- squared paper
- ruler
- coloured pencils

**Challenge 1**

The pictogram shows the number of bottles of sunscreen sold by Busy Chemists in one week.

**Sales of sunscreen**

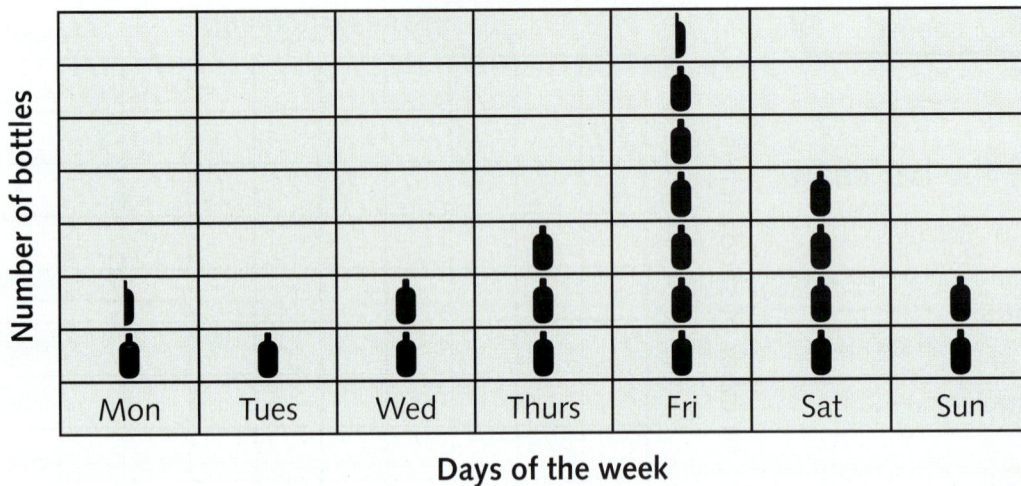

Number of bottles

Mon | Tues | Wed | Thurs | Fri | Sat | Sun

**Days of the week**

**Key**

🧴 2 bottles

❘ 1 bottle

1. Copy the table. Write the number of bottles that were sold each day.

| Day | Number |
|-----------|--------|
| Monday | |
| Tuesday | |
| Wednesday | |
| Thursday | |
| Friday | |
| Saturday | |
| Sunday | |

2. a  Which day had the fewest sales?

   b  Which two days had the same number of sales?

   c  How many more bottles were sold on Friday than on Monday?

3. Why do you think that Friday had the most sales of sunscreen?

The pictogram shows how often the call centre holidays4u was called in one day.

**holidays4u calls**

| Time period | | | | | | | |
|---|---|---|---|---|---|---|---|
| 7a.m.–9a.m. | ✳ | ✳ | ✳ | ✳ | ✳ | ✳ | ✳ |
| 9a.m.–11a.m. | ✳ | ✳ | ✳ | ＊ | | | |
| 11a.m.–1p.m. | ✳ | ✳ | ✳ | | | | |
| 1p.m.–3p.m. | ＊ | | | | | | |
| 3p.m.–5p.m. | ✳ | ✳ | ✳ | ✳ | | | |
| 5p.m.–7p.m. | ✳ | ✳ | | | | | |
| 7p.m.–9p.m. | ✳ | ✳ | ✳ | ✳ | ✳ | ＊ | |

Number of calls

**Key**

✳ 2 calls

＊ 1 call

**1** Draw a table to show the number of times the call centre was phoned in each 2-hour period.

**2 a** How many calls did the call centre get altogether?

**b** Which 2-hour period had the fewest visits?

**c** During which 2-hour periods were there more than seven calls to the call centre?

**d** How many more calls were made between 7p.m. and 9p.m. than between 9a.m. and 11a.m.?

**1 a** Draw a bar chart for the data in the holidays4u calls pictogram.

**b** How many fewer calls were made between 5p.m. and 7p.m. than between 7a.m. and 9a.m.?

**c** Which two 2-hour periods had the most calls? Explain why you think this is the case.

**2** Write two statements about the data in your bar chart.

# Counting in steps of 50 and 100

- Count on and back in multiples of 50 and 100
- Find 100 more or less than a number

**Challenge 1**

Write the missing numbers in each row.

| a | 55 | 60 | | 70 | | | | | | | | |
|---|----|----|--|----|--|--|--|--|--|--|--|--|
| b | 110 | | | 140 | | | | | 190 | | | |
| c | 50 | | | | 250 | | | | | 500 | | |
| d | 100 | | | | | | 700 | | | 1,000 | | |

**Challenge 2**

Find the number of the spaceship by following the footprints. Start on 0 and be careful of the craters!

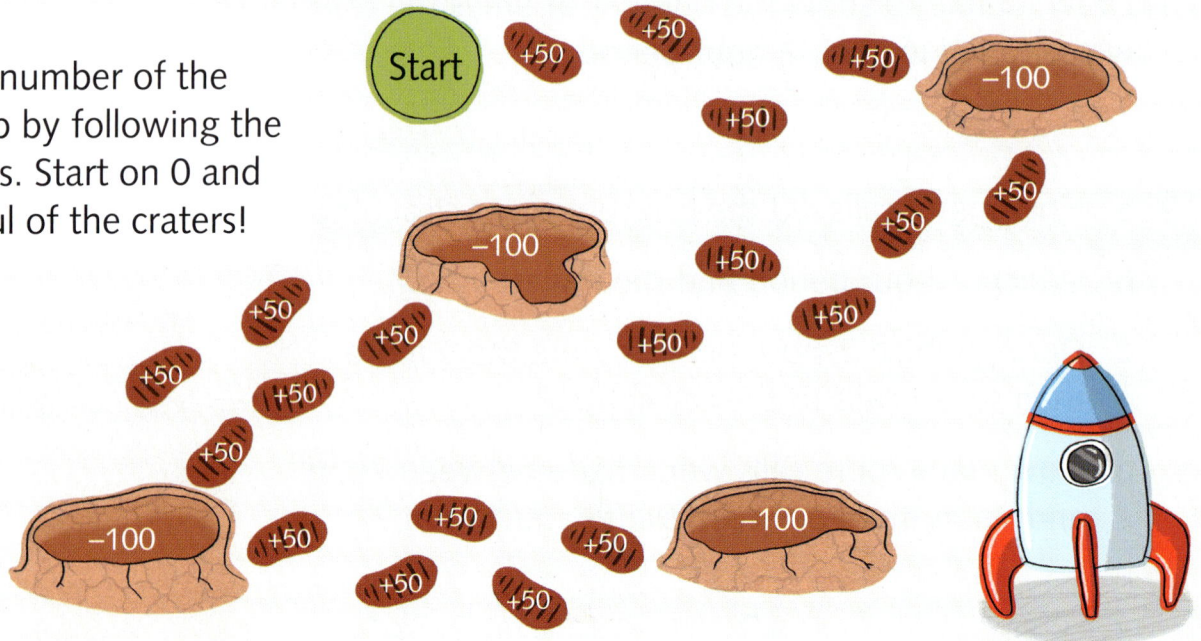

Start
+50 +50 +50 +50 −100
+50 +50
−100 +50 +50
+50 +50 +50 +50
+50 +50
+50 +50
−100 +50 +50 +50 −100
+50 +50

**Challenge 3**

Stars: 25  145  360  400  53  321  299  1

Moon rocks: 785  651  600  602  853  999  872  748

1 Choose a start number from the stars. Count forwards from your start number in steps of 100. Continue the count for 6 numbers. Repeat for each start number on the stars.

2 Choose a start number from the moon rocks. Count backwards from your start number in steps of 100. Continue the count for 6 numbers. Repeat for each start number on the moon rocks.

# Revising multiplication facts

Consolidate recall of the multiplication facts for the 2, 3, 4, 5, 8 and 10 multiplication tables, and related facts involving multiples of 10

**Challenge 1**

Write a multiplication fact for each number coming out of the machine.

a  6
   3
   7  ×4
   4
   9

b  9
   5
   8  ×3
   3
   6

c  5
   6
   9  ×8
   4
   7

**Challenge 2**

Find the missing digit, or digits, in each calculation.

a  $3 \times 9 = 2$☆

b  $4 \times$ ☆ $= 28$

c  ☆ $\times 8 = 32$

d  ☆ $\times 4 = 16$

e  $7 \times 5 =$ ☆$5$

f  $6 \times$ ☆ $= 24$

g  $8 \times 8 =$ ☆$4$

h  $6 \times$ ☆ $=$ ☆$8$

i  $1$☆ $\times$ ☆ $= 48$

j  $9 \times$ ☆ $= 4$☆

k  ☆ $\times 8 = 6$☆

l  $9 \times$ ☆ $= 3$☆

**Challenge 3**

1  Follow the rules to calculate the score for each dart thrown.

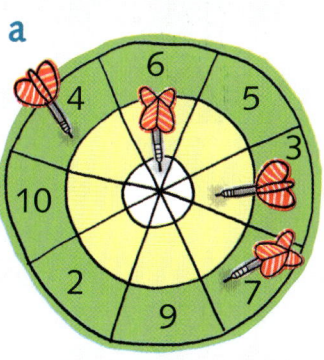

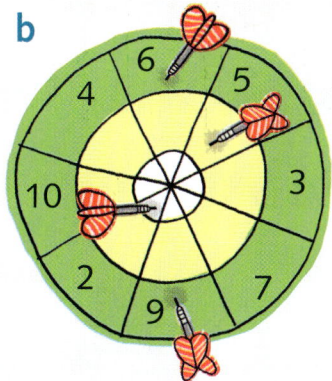

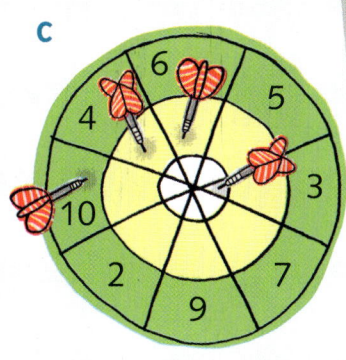

Dart rules:
white: ×80
yellow: ×30
green: ×40

a

b

c

2  For each dartboard, add together the four darts to find the total score. Which dartboard scored the most points?

# Revising division facts

Consolidate recall of the division facts for the 2, 3, 4, 5, 8 and 10 multiplication tables, and related facts involving multiples of 10

**Challenge 1**

Write a division fact for each number coming out of the machine.

a  36
   12
   27
   24
   9
   ÷3

b  24
   56
   48
   32
   16
   ÷8

c  12
   36
   20
   44
   32
   ÷4

**Challenge 2**

Look at the number sentences on either side of the boxes.
Use the symbols <, = or > to make each number sentence true.

a  $45 \div 5$        $36 \div 3$
b  $64 \div 8$        $32 \div 4$
c  $48 \div 8$        $36 \div 4$
d  $56 \div 8$        $48 \div 4$
e  $18 \div 3$        $28 \div 4$
f  $50 \div 10$       $80 \div 8$

**Challenge 3**

**1** Find the missing digit, or digits, in each calculation.

a  $36 \div 9 = \bigcirc$

b  $48 \div \triangle = 12$

c  $\square \div 4 = 9$

d  $21 \div 3 = \blacksquare$

e  $\bigcirc 4 \div 8 = 8$

f  $\triangle 6 \div \bigcirc = 2$

g  $2\bigcirc \div \triangle = 5$

h  $6\triangle \div \blacksquare = 12$

i  $3\square \div 8 = \bigcirc$

**2** a  $360 \div 4 = \bigcirc$

b  $280 \div 4 = \blacksquare$

c  $\bigcirc \div 3 = 90$

d  $210 \div 3 = \square$

e  $320 \div 8 = \triangle$

f  $160 \div \square = 40$

g  $240 \div \triangle = 30$

h  $640 \div \bigcirc = 80$

i  $350 \div \triangle = 70$

# Solving word problems (6)

## Solve word problems and reason mathematically

**Challenge 1**

Write a multiplication and division fact for each of these pictures.

a [16]  b [20]  c [25]  d [21]

**Example**

[24]

$24 \div 3 = 8$
$8 \times 3 = 24$

**Challenge 2**

Read the clues to find the numbers.

a It is twelve times larger than 4.

b It is double 8 and 4 more.

c It is 20 times larger than 3 multiplied by 2.

d It is double 8 and double 8 again.

e It is 5 less than 25 divided by 5.

f It is 5 times more than 9.

g It is half of 64 and half again.

h It is the sum of 40 divided by 8 and 24 divided by 4.

i It is the same as 9 multiplied by 4 and 3 multiplied by 12.

**Challenge 3**

a Nabil has 64 stamps. Amal has 8 stamps. How many times more stamps does Nabil have than Amal?

b 56 cars are in the car park in the morning. Half are gone by lunchtime. How many are left?

c A pizza is split into slices and eaten. Johan eats 8 slices of pizza and May eats 12 slices of pizza. How many slices in the whole pizza?

d A cook bakes 40 biscuits. He needs to bake 8 times more. How many biscuits does he need in total?

e 27 cakes are shared between 9 children. How many for each child? If cakes cost 40p each, how much did each child pay?

# Compare and order fractions

Compare and order unit fractions and fractions with the same denominator

**Challenge 1**

**1** Write the larger fraction in each pair.

a $\frac{1}{4}$ ▭ $\frac{1}{2}$ ▭    b $\frac{1}{10}$ ▭ $\frac{1}{8}$ ▭    c $\frac{1}{4}$ ▭ $\frac{1}{5}$ ▭

**2** Copy and complete, writing <, = or > between each pair of fractions.

a $\frac{3}{4}$ $\frac{1}{4}$    b $\frac{3}{5}$ $\frac{4}{5}$    c $\frac{6}{10}$ $\frac{3}{10}$

d $\frac{1}{5}$ $\frac{1}{2}$    e $\frac{1}{6}$ $\frac{1}{9}$    f $\frac{1}{10}$ $\frac{1}{8}$

**Challenge 2**

**1** Order each set of fractions, smallest to largest.

a $\frac{5}{7}, \frac{2}{7}, \frac{6}{7}, \frac{1}{7}$    b $\frac{3}{10}, \frac{6}{10}, \frac{2}{10}, \frac{5}{10}$

c $\frac{7}{8}, \frac{4}{8}, \frac{3}{8}, \frac{6}{8}$    d $\frac{1}{5}, \frac{1}{10}, \frac{1}{6}, \frac{1}{4}$

e $\frac{1}{4}, \frac{1}{7}, \frac{1}{9}, \frac{1}{2}$    f $\frac{1}{8}, \frac{1}{3}, \frac{1}{12}, \frac{1}{5}$

**2** Draw a number line to order each set of fractions.

a $\frac{4}{9}, \frac{7}{9}, \frac{3}{9}, \frac{6}{9}$    b $\frac{2}{6}, \frac{5}{6}, \frac{1}{6}, \frac{4}{6}$

c $\frac{7}{12}, \frac{5}{12}, \frac{11}{12}, \frac{2}{12}$    d $\frac{1}{6}, \frac{1}{10}, \frac{1}{3}, \frac{1}{7}$

e $\frac{1}{11}, \frac{1}{8}, \frac{1}{2}, \frac{1}{5}$    f $\frac{1}{5}, \frac{1}{12}, \frac{1}{9}, \frac{1}{3}$

**Challenge 3**

Copy and complete, writing the missing fractions on each number line.

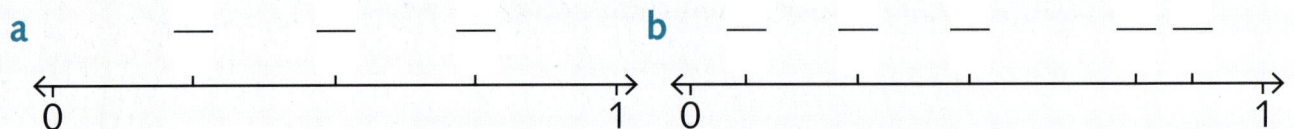

a $\underline{\quad}$ $\underline{\quad}$ $\underline{\quad}$    b $\underline{\quad}$ $\underline{\quad}$ $\underline{\quad}$ $\underline{\quad}$ $\underline{\quad}$

0 ———————————— 1    0 ———————————— 1

# Subtracting fractions

Subtract fractions within one whole

**You will need:**
- interlocking cubes of 2 different colours
- coloured pencils

**llenge 1** Make a model using 6 cubes in two different colours. Put cubes of the same colour together.

**Example**

$\frac{6}{6} - \frac{1}{6} = \frac{5}{6}$

a Draw it in your book.

b Write a fraction subtraction to show the answer when the cubes of one colour are removed from the whole model.

c Repeat the above twice more with different numbers of each colour.

**llenge 2**

1 Look at these models. Write a fraction subtraction to show the answer when the cubes of one colour are removed from the whole model.

a    b    c 

d    e    f 

2 a $\frac{3}{4} - \frac{1}{4} =$   b $\frac{3}{4} - \frac{2}{4} =$   c $\frac{7}{8} - \frac{1}{8} =$   d $\frac{2}{3} - \frac{1}{3} =$

e $\frac{7}{8} - \frac{3}{8} =$   f $\frac{3}{5} - \frac{2}{5} =$   g $\frac{3}{6} - \frac{1}{6} =$   h $\frac{3}{7} - \frac{2}{7} =$

i $\frac{7}{9} - \frac{2}{9} =$   j $\frac{7}{10} - \frac{4}{10} =$   k $\frac{5}{7} - \frac{3}{7} =$   l $\frac{3}{10} - \frac{2}{10} =$

**lenge 3**

1 a $\frac{7}{9} - \frac{\quad}{\quad} = \frac{5}{9}$   b $\frac{\quad}{\quad} - \frac{2}{7} = \frac{1}{7}$   c $\frac{4}{5} - \frac{\quad}{\quad} = \frac{3}{5}$

d $\frac{5}{8} - \frac{\quad}{\quad} = \frac{3}{8}$   e $\frac{8}{12} - \frac{\quad}{\quad} = \frac{5}{12}$   f $\frac{\quad}{\quad} - \frac{2}{10} = \frac{7}{10}$

2 Explain why $\frac{8}{8}$ is the same as 1 whole.

# Equivalent fractions

## Recognise equivalent fractions

**You will need:**
- interlocking cubes of two different colours
- coloured pencils

**Challenge 1**

Using cubes, make some models that can join the Half Club. They need to be half one colour and half another colour.

Draw the models and complete this sentence for each model:

$\frac{1}{2}$ of my model is [ ] and $\frac{1}{2}$ of my model is [ ].

See how many different models you can make.

**Challenge 2**

Using cubes, make some models that can join the Half Club.

Draw the models and write the fraction that is equivalent to half for each one.

Make 10 different models.

**Example**

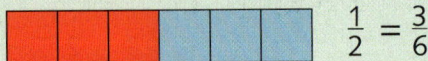 $\frac{1}{2} = \frac{3}{6}$

**Challenge 3**

1 What does 'equivalent' mean?

2 Draw some models, and write the fractions, that are equivalent to $\frac{1}{3}$, $\frac{1}{4}$ and $\frac{1}{5}$.

This model is $\frac{1}{4}$ purple, so it joins the One-quarter Club.

**Example**

$\frac{1}{4} = \frac{2}{8}$

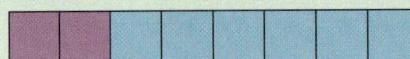

# Fractions wall

Recognise equivalent fractions

Challenge 1

You will need:
• three equal strips of paper

1 Fold three strips of paper to make a fraction wall.

   a   Fold one strip in half.

   b   Fold another strip to show quarters.

   c   Fold the remaining strip to show eighths.

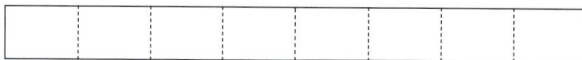

2 Stick them into your exercise book, making sure the middle folds all line up.

3 What fractions can you see that are the same? Record them like this: $\frac{1}{2} = \frac{2}{4}$.

Challenge 2

You will need:
• five equal strips of paper

1 Fold five strips of paper to make a fraction wall. Make halves, quarters, sixths, eighths and tenths.

2 Stick them into your exercise book, making sure the middle folds all line up.

3 What fractions can you see that are the same? Record them like this: $\frac{1}{4} = \frac{2}{8}$.

I can see that $\frac{1}{2}$ and $\frac{2}{4}$ are the same.

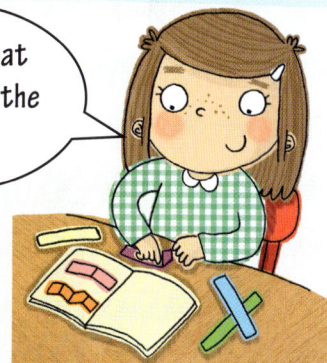

Challenge 3

You will need:
• seven equal strips of paper

1 Fold seven strips of paper to make a fraction wall. Make halves, thirds, quarters, sixths, eighths, tenths and twelfths.

   a   What fractions can you see that are the same? Record them like this: $\frac{1}{3} = \frac{2}{6}$.

   b   Which fraction strips were the hardest to fold? Explain why.

# Perimeters of rectangles

Calculate the perimeter of rectangles in centimetres and metres

**Example**

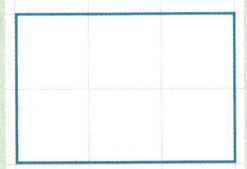

perimeter
= 3 cm + 2 cm + 3 cm + 2 cm
= 10 cm

**Challenge 1**

Find the perimeter of each rectangle in centimetres.

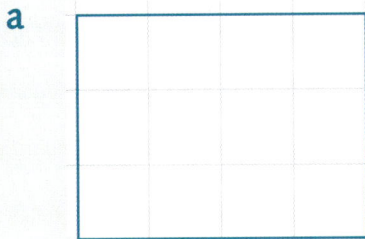

a

b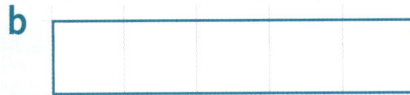

**Challenge 2**

1  The dots are 1 cm apart. Find the perimeter of each rectangle in centimetres.

a    b    c

2  Write the perimeter of each vegetable bed A to E in metres.

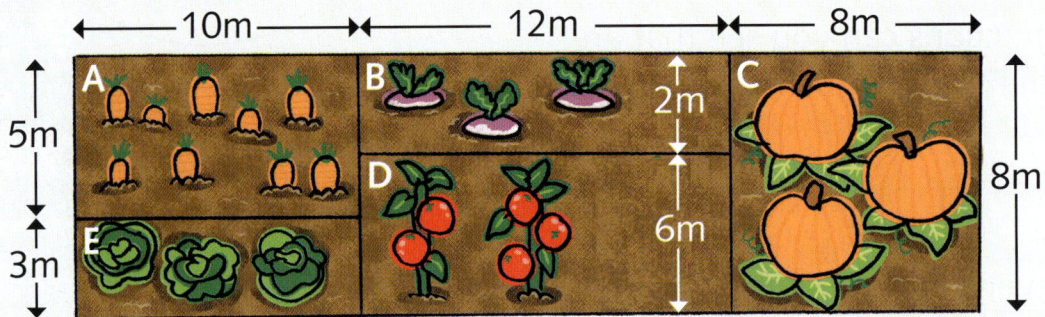

**Challenge 3**

Monty needs more space to grow salads and potatoes. He joins vegetable beds A and E in Challenge 2 to make one bed for salads, and beds B and D for potatoes. Find the perimeter of:

a  the new bed for salads

b  the new bed for potatoes

# Drawing and calculating perimeters

## Using a ruler, draw and calculate the perimeter of rectangles

**Challenge 1**

On 1 cm squared paper draw different rectangles with perimeters of:

a  10 cm     b  14 cm

c  18 cm

**Example**

perimeter = 12 cm

**You will need:**
- ruler
- 1 cm squared paper

**Challenges 2, 3**

On 1 cm square dot grid paper draw a square then all the rectangles which have a perimeter of:

a  4 cm     b  8 cm

c  12 cm    d  16 cm

e  20 cm

**Example**

perimeter = 14 cm

**You will need:**
- ruler
- 1 cm square dot grid paper

**Challenge 3**

Do Challenge 2 then copy and complete the table.

**You will need:**
- ruler
- 1 cm square dot grid paper

| Side of square | Perimeter of square | Number of rectangles with same perimeter | Total number of squares and rectangles |
|---|---|---|---|
| 1 cm | 4 cm | 0 | 1 |
| 2 cm | 8 cm | | |
| 3 cm | | | |
| 4 cm | | | |
| 5 cm | | | |

# Regular perimeters

## Measure and calculate the perimeter of 2-D shapes

**You will need:**
• ruler

**Challenge 1**

Use your ruler to measure the perimeter of these regular shapes in centimetres.

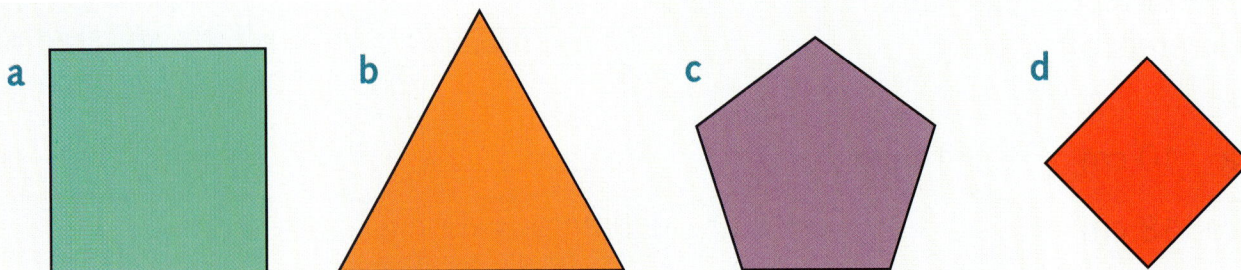

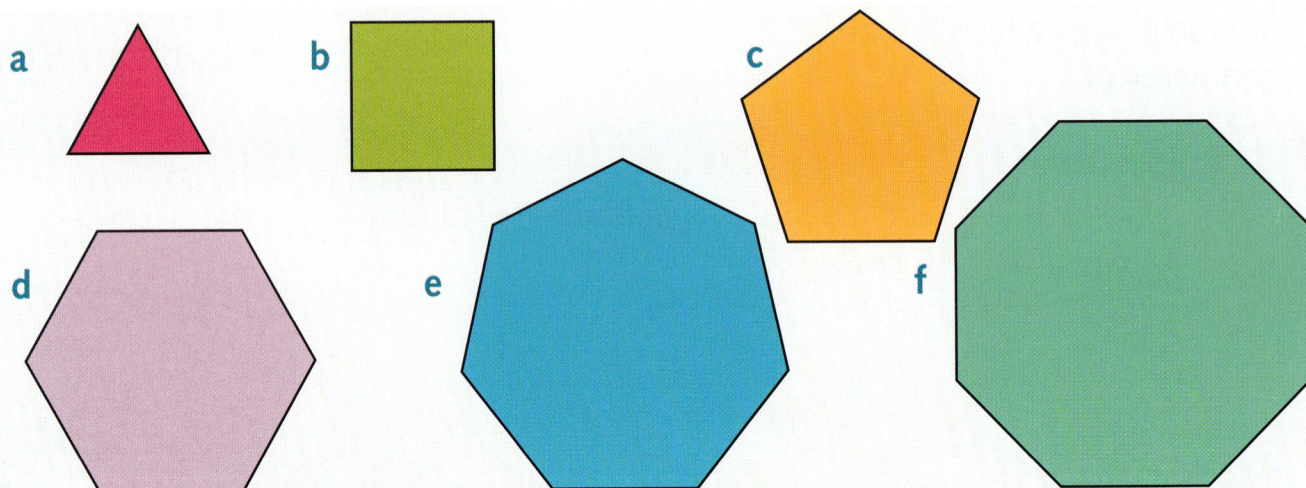

a   b   c   d

**Challenges 2, 3**

Use your ruler to measure the perimeter of these regular shapes in centimetres.

a   b   c

d   e   f

1   Copy and complete the table for the regular shapes in Challenges 2, 3.

| Number of sides of shape | 3 | 4 | 5 | 6 | 7 | 8 |
|---|---|---|---|---|---|---|
| Perimeter in centimetres | | | | | | |

2   If you continue the pattern, what will the perimeter of these regular shapes measure?

a   10 sides          b   12 sides

54

# Perimeters of 2-D shapes

## Measure and calculate the perimeter of 2-D shapes

**You will need:**
- four to five square tiles
- 1 cm squared paper
- ruler
- coloured pencils

**Challenge 1**

1 Make each shape with four square tiles then draw the shape on to 1 cm squared paper.

a     b     c     d

2 Below each shape, write its perimeter.

**Challenge 2**

1 Make each shape with five square tiles then draw the shape on to 1 cm squared paper.

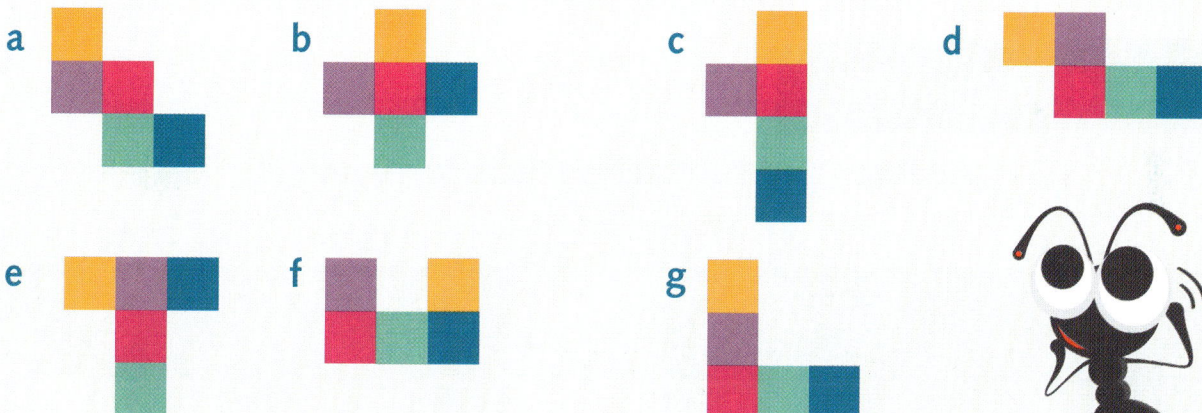

a     b     c     d

e     f     g

2 Below each shape, write its perimeter.

**Challenge 3**

With five squares, you can make 12 different shapes. Seven of the shapes are drawn in Challenge 2.

1 Find the remaining five shapes.

2 Draw them on to 1 cm squared paper and calculate their perimeters.

# Maths facts

## Problem solving

**The seven steps to solving word problems**
**1** Read the problem carefully.    **2** What do you have to find?
**3** What facts are given?    **4** Which of the facts do you need?    **5** Make a plan.
**6** Carry out your plan to obtain your answer.    **7** Check your answer.

## Number and place value

| 100 | 200 | 300 | 400 | 500 | 600 | 700 | 800 | 900 |
|-----|-----|-----|-----|-----|-----|-----|-----|-----|
| 10 | 20 | 30 | 40 | 50 | 60 | 70 | 80 | 90 |
| 1 | 2 | 3 | 4 | 5 | 6 | 7 | 8 | 9 |

## Addition and subtraction

### Addition and subtraction facts to 10 and 20

| + | 0 | 1 | 2 | 3 | 4 | 5 | 6 | 7 | 8 | 9 | 10 |
|---|---|---|---|---|---|---|---|---|---|---|----|
| 0 | 0 | 1 | 2 | 3 | 4 | 5 | 6 | 7 | 8 | 9 | 10 |
| 1 | 1 | 2 | 3 | 4 | 5 | 6 | 7 | 8 | 9 | 10 | 11 |
| 2 | 2 | 3 | 4 | 5 | 6 | 7 | 8 | 9 | 10 | 11 | 12 |
| 3 | 3 | 4 | 5 | 6 | 7 | 8 | 9 | 10 | 11 | 12 | 13 |
| 4 | 4 | 5 | 6 | 7 | 8 | 9 | 10 | 11 | 12 | 13 | 14 |
| 5 | 5 | 6 | 7 | 8 | 9 | 10 | 11 | 12 | 13 | 14 | 15 |
| 6 | 6 | 7 | 8 | 9 | 10 | 11 | 12 | 13 | 14 | 15 | 16 |
| 7 | 7 | 8 | 9 | 10 | 11 | 12 | 13 | 14 | 15 | 16 | 17 |
| 8 | 8 | 9 | 10 | 11 | 12 | 13 | 14 | 15 | 16 | 17 | 18 |
| 9 | 9 | 10 | 11 | 12 | 13 | 14 | 15 | 16 | 17 | 18 | 19 |
| 10 | 10 | 11 | 12 | 13 | 14 | 15 | 16 | 17 | 18 | 19 | 20 |

| + | 11 | 12 | 13 | 14 | 15 | 16 | 17 | 18 | 19 | 20 |
|---|----|----|----|----|----|----|----|----|----|----|
| 0 | 11 | 12 | 13 | 14 | 15 | 16 | 17 | 18 | 19 | 20 |
| 1 | 12 | 13 | 14 | 15 | 16 | 17 | 18 | 19 | 20 | |
| 2 | 13 | 14 | 15 | 16 | 17 | 18 | 19 | 20 | | |
| 3 | 14 | 15 | 16 | 17 | 18 | 19 | 20 | | | |
| 4 | 15 | 16 | 17 | 18 | 19 | 20 | | | | |
| 5 | 16 | 17 | 18 | 19 | 20 | | | | | |
| 6 | 17 | 18 | 19 | 20 | | | | | | |
| 7 | 18 | 19 | 20 | | | | | | | |
| 8 | 19 | 20 | | | | | | | | |
| 9 | 20 | | | | | | | | | |

# Multiples of 10 addition and subtraction facts

| +   | 0   | 10  | 20  | 30  | 40  | 50  | 60  | 70  | 80  | 90  | 100 |
|-----|-----|-----|-----|-----|-----|-----|-----|-----|-----|-----|-----|
| 0   | 0   | 10  | 20  | 30  | 40  | 50  | 60  | 70  | 80  | 90  | 100 |
| 10  | 10  | 20  | 30  | 40  | 50  | 60  | 70  | 80  | 90  | 100 | 110 |
| 20  | 20  | 30  | 40  | 50  | 60  | 70  | 80  | 90  | 100 | 110 | 120 |
| 30  | 30  | 40  | 50  | 60  | 70  | 80  | 90  | 100 | 110 | 120 | 130 |
| 40  | 40  | 50  | 60  | 70  | 80  | 90  | 100 | 110 | 120 | 130 | 140 |
| 50  | 50  | 60  | 70  | 80  | 90  | 100 | 110 | 120 | 130 | 140 | 150 |
| 60  | 60  | 70  | 80  | 90  | 100 | 110 | 120 | 130 | 140 | 150 | 160 |
| 70  | 70  | 80  | 90  | 100 | 110 | 120 | 130 | 140 | 150 | 160 | 170 |
| 80  | 80  | 90  | 100 | 110 | 120 | 130 | 140 | 150 | 160 | 170 | 180 |
| 90  | 90  | 100 | 110 | 120 | 130 | 140 | 150 | 160 | 170 | 180 | 190 |
| 100 | 100 | 110 | 120 | 130 | 140 | 150 | 160 | 170 | 180 | 190 | 200 |

## Written methods – addition

Example: 548 + 387

**Expanded written method**

```
   5 4 8
 + 3 8 7
 ───────
    1 5
  1 2 0
  8 0 0
 ───────
  9 3 5
 ───────
```

**Formal written method**

```
   5 4 8
 + 3 8 7
 ───────
   9 3 5
 ───────
   1 1
```

## Written methods – subtraction

Example: 582 – 237

**Expanded written method**

```
              70    12
    500      8̶0    2̶
  − 200      30    7
  ────────────────────
    300      40    5
```

300 + 40 + 5 = 345

**Formal written method**

```
      7  1
    5 8̶ 2
  − 2 3 7
  ───────
    3 4 5
```

You can also write the exchanged values like this.

```
      7  12
    5 8̶ 2
  − 2 3 7
  ───────
    3 4 5
```

# Multiplication and division

## Multiplication and division facts

| × | 2 | 3 | 4 | 5 | 8 | 10 |
|---|---|---|---|---|---|---|
| 1 | 2 | 3 | 4 | 5 | 8 | 10 |
| 2 | 4 | 6 | 8 | 10 | 16 | 20 |
| 3 | 6 | 9 | 12 | 15 | 24 | 30 |
| 4 | 8 | 12 | 16 | 20 | 32 | 40 |
| 5 | 10 | 15 | 20 | 25 | 40 | 50 |
| 6 | 12 | 18 | 24 | 30 | 48 | 60 |
| 7 | 14 | 21 | 28 | 35 | 56 | 70 |
| 8 | 16 | 24 | 32 | 40 | 64 | 80 |
| 9 | 18 | 27 | 36 | 45 | 72 | 90 |
| 10 | 20 | 30 | 40 | 50 | 80 | 100 |
| 11 | 22 | 33 | 44 | 55 | 88 | 110 |
| 12 | 24 | 36 | 48 | 60 | 96 | 120 |

## Multiples of 10 multiplication and division facts

| × | 1 | 2 | 3 | 4 | 5 | 6 | 7 | 8 | 9 | 10 | 11 | 12 |
|---|---|---|---|---|---|---|---|---|---|---|---|---|
| 20 | 20 | 40 | 60 | 80 | 100 | 120 | 140 | 160 | 180 | 200 | 220 | 240 |
| 30 | 30 | 60 | 90 | 120 | 150 | 180 | 210 | 240 | 270 | 300 | 330 | 360 |
| 40 | 40 | 80 | 120 | 160 | 200 | 240 | 280 | 320 | 360 | 400 | 440 | 480 |
| 50 | 50 | 100 | 150 | 200 | 250 | 300 | 350 | 400 | 450 | 500 | 550 | 600 |
| 80 | 80 | 160 | 240 | 320 | 400 | 480 | 560 | 640 | 720 | 800 | 880 | 960 |
| 100 | 100 | 200 | 300 | 400 | 500 | 600 | 700 | 800 | 900 | 1,000 | 1,100 | 1,200 |

## Written methods – multiplication

Example: $63 \times 8$

**Partitioning**

$63 \times 8 = (60 \times 8) + (3 \times 8)$
$= 480 + 24$
$= 504$

**Grid method**

| × | 60 | 3 | |
|---|---|---|---|
| 8 | 480 | 24 | = 504 |

**Expanded written method**

```
    6 3
  ×   8
    2 4   (3 × 8)
  4 8 0   (60 × 8)
  5 0 4
    1
```

**Formal written method**

```
    6 3          6 3
  ×   8      ×  ₂ 8
  5 0 4        5 0 4
    2
```

You can also write the regrouped value like this.

## Written methods – division

Example: $92 \div 4$

**Partitioning**

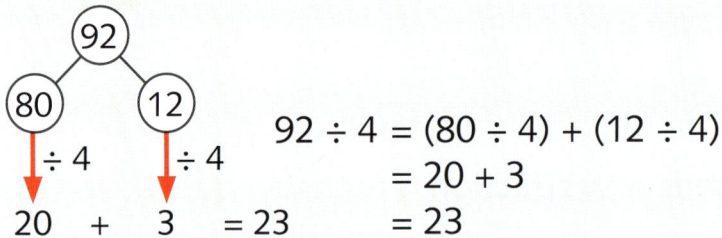

$92 \div 4 = (80 \div 4) + (12 \div 4)$
$= 20 + 3$
$= 23$

**Expanded written method**

```
    2 3
  4)9 2
  − 8 0   (20 × 4)
    1 2
  − 1 2   (3 × 4)
      0
```

**Formal written method**

```
    2 3
  4) 9 ¹2
```

You can also include the related multiplication facts.

## Fractions

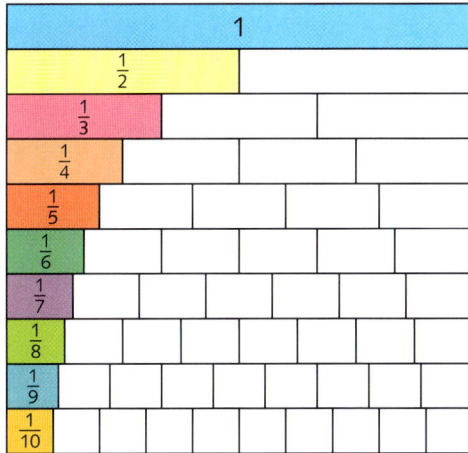

## Measurement

### Length
1 metre (m) = 100 centimetres (cm) = 1,000 millimetres (mm)

### Mass
1 kilogram (kg) = 1,000 grams (g)

### Capacity
1 litre (*l*) = 1,000 millilitres (ml)

### Time

| | | |
|---|---|---|
| 1 year | = | 12 months |
| | = | 365 days |
| | = | 366 days (leap year) |
| 1 week | = | 7 days |
| 1 day | = | 24 hours |
| 1 hour | = | 60 minutes |
| 1 minute | = | 60 seconds |

12-hour clock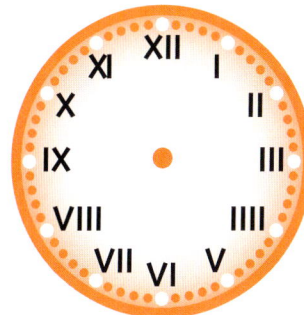

24-hour clock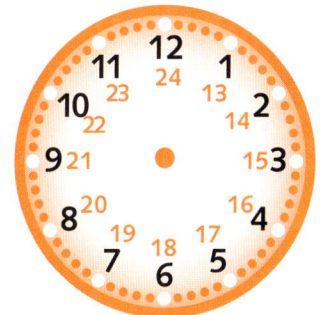

## Properties of shape

right-angled triangle    equilateral triangle    isosceles triangle    scalene triangle

 circle    semi-circle    square    rectangle    pentagon    hexagon    heptagon    octagon

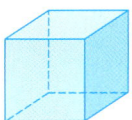 cube    cuboid    cone    cylinder    sphere 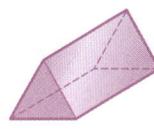 triangular prism    triangular-based pyramid (tetrahedron)    square-based pyramid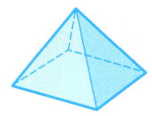

William Collins' dream of knowledge for all began with the publication of his first book in 1819.

A self-educated mill worker, he not only enriched millions of lives, but also founded a flourishing publishing house. Today, staying true to this spirit, Collins books are packed with inspiration, innovation and practical expertise.

They place you at the centre of a world of possibility and give you exactly what you need to explore it.

Collins. Freedom to teach.

Published by Collins

An imprint of HarperCollins*Publishers*
The News Building, 1 London Bridge Street, London, SE1 9GF, UK

HarperCollins*Publishers*
Macken House, 39/40 Mayor Street Upper, Dublin 1, D01 C9W8, Ireland

> Browse the complete Collins catalogue at
> **collins.co.uk**

10 9 8 7 6 5 4 3 2 1

ISBN 978-0-00-861335-8

British Library Cataloguing-in-Publication Data

A catalogue record for this publication is available from the British Library.

Series editor: Peter Clarke
Cover design and artwork: Amparo Barrera
Internal design concept: Amparo Barrera
Designer: Niki Merrett
Typesetter: David Jimenez
Illustrators: Louise Forshaw, Steven Woods, Gwyneth Williamson and Eva Sassin
Printed and bound in Great Britain by Martins the Printers

FSC™
www.fsc.org
**MIX**
Paper | Supporting responsible forestry
**FSC™ C007454**

This book is produced from independently certified FSC™ paper to ensure responsible forest management.

For more information visit: harpercollins.co.uk/green

> Busy Ant Maths 2nd edition components are compatible with the 1st edition of Busy Ant Maths.